D0895858

THE
POWER
OF
DREAMS

© Warren H. McLemore

About the Author

Joe H. Slate is a licensed psychologist in private practice and emeritus professor of psychology at Athens State University (ASU), where he served as professor of psychology, head of behavioral sciences, and director of institutional effectiveness. He holds a PhD from the University of Alabama with postdoctoral studies at the University of California. He is a member of the American Psychological Association and a Platinum Registrant in the National Register of Health Service Psychologists.

As head of the behavioral sciences at Athens State University, Slate established the university's parapsychology and biofeedback research laboratory and introduced biofeedback, hypnosis, dream power, and paranormal phenomena into the curriculum. His research includes projects for the US Army, the Parapsychology Foundation (New York), and numerous private sources.

With the assistance of Dr. James E. Bathurst, the university's former academic dean and emeritus professor of psychology, Slate helped organize in 1970 the parapsychology club that later became known as the Parapsychology Research Institute and Foundation (PRIF) at Athens State University (then College). PRIF was designed for the express purpose of promoting the scientific study of parapsychology and the endowment of student scholarships. As head of the behavioral sciences, he became instrumental in promoting a vigorous research program and establishing student scholarships in perpetuity. Following his retirement from Athens State University in 1992, PRIF became a non-college-affiliated group that continued its vigorous research and foundation efforts.

He is the author of eighteen books and coauthor of sixteen books with Carl Llewellyn Weschcke. In addition to dream power, his research interests include health and fitness, rejuvenation, astral projection, hypnosis, learning, psychotherapy, self-empowerment, and the afterlife, to list but a few.

THE

POWER

OF

DREAMS

*How to Interpret & Focus the Energy
of Your Subconscious Mind*

JOE H. SLATE PhD

Llewellyn Publications
Woodbury, Minnesota

The Power of Dreams: How to Interpret & Focus the Energy of Your Subconscious Mind © 2018 by Joe H. Slate, PhD. All rights reserved. No part of this book may be used or reproduced in any manner whatsoever, including Internet usage, without written permission from Llewellyn Publications, except in the case of brief quotations embodied in critical articles and reviews.

First Edition
First Printing, 2018

Cover design by Kevin R. Brown
Interior art by Llewellyn Art Department

Llewellyn Publications is a registered trademark of Llewellyn Worldwide Ltd.

Library of Congress Cataloging-in-Publication Data (Pending)
ISBN: 978-0-7387-5189-4

Llewellyn Worldwide Ltd. does not participate in, endorse, or have any authority or responsibility concerning private business transactions between our authors and the public.

All mail addressed to the author is forwarded but the publisher cannot, unless specifically instructed by the author, give out an address or phone number.

Any Internet references contained in this work are current at publication time, but the publisher cannot guarantee that a specific location will continue to be maintained. Please refer to the publisher's website for links to authors' websites and other sources.

Llewellyn Publications
A Division of Llewellyn Worldwide Ltd.
2143 Wooddale Drive
Woodbury, MN 55125-2989
www.llewellyn.com

Printed in the United States of America

Other Books by Joe H. Slate, PhD

Aura Energy for Health, Healing & Balance
Connecting to the Power of Nature
Psychic Vampires
Rejuvenation

Cowritten with Carl Llewellyn Weschcke

Astral Projection and Psychic Empowerment
Clairvoyance for Psychic Empowerment
Communicating with Spirit
Doors to Past Lives & Future Lives
The Llewellyn Complete Book of Psychic Empowerment
The New Science of the Paranormal
Psychic Empowerment for Everyone
Self-Empowerment through Self-Hypnosis
Self-Empowerment and Your Subconscious Mind

© Lisa Novak

This book is dedicated to the late Carl Llewellyn Weschcke,
who became known worldwide as the Father of the New Age.

Contents

Disclaimer

Certain preparatory considerations are essential to the effective application of the numerous self-administered programs and techniques presented throughout this book. A preview of the full program and familiarity with each step are essential to the program's effectiveness. Each program requires a safe, secure setting free of distraction or interruption. The programs and specific techniques related to them are not designed for use while driving, operating machinery, or engaging in other activities requiring concentration or focused attention.

Foreword:
The Value and Purpose
of Dreamtime

Carl Llewellyn Weschcke

Awake or Asleep—Pay Attention!
We spend about a third of our lives seemingly **"asleep at the switch"**—basically meaning we aren't paying attention!
Paying attention to what?

We think of sleep primarily in terms of providing rest and recuperation for the physical body, and many people think of the accompanying dream state as—at best—a kind of unconscious entertainment and at worst a scary "nightmare" that wakes us up.

Same question: *Paying attention to what? And how?* We surely know what *"asleep at the wheel"* means—that is, if we didn't die in a resultant car accident. We know that survival and accomplishment depend upon an alert mind and focused consciousness. We pay attention to what we are doing and to *what we are going to do*. We plan ahead and we set goals. We live twenty-four hours a day and our consciousness is active—in many different ways—all twenty-four hours.

We commonly divide our twenty-four-hour day into two major eight-hour parts: (1) daytime for wide-awake activities, mostly work related; and (2) nighttime for rest and sleep. Between those two we have morning and evening intervals for meals, playtime, checking the news, and so-called *leisure* activities, which hopefully include reading and study of Llewellyn books and practice of their subject matter.

And then there is **DREAMTIME.**

Many have a mistaken view of "consciousness" as something to turn on and off. Sleep is a state of consciousness; the awake (or conscious) mind is a state of consciousness, dreaming is a state of consciousness—as also is meditation, magick, prayer, concentration, hypnosis, going out-of-body, rising on the planes, sexual orgasm and other forms of ecstasy, and many more, all involving different *focus* and *vibratory patterns* of consciousness. Even in physical death there is no loss of consciousness, only a changed state.

We are mind and spirit, and all is consciousness. In our learning, our studies, and our practices we develop skills for using consciousness to accomplish predetermined goals.

And in the broad spectrum of consciousness spanning the cosmos there are many dream states.

The Variety and Complexity of Dreams

As one early researcher observed,[1] our attempt to catalog the many types of dreams and their origin, content, meaning, purpose, function, value, relations to altered states of consciousness, connections to levels of conscious and unconscious life, memories of this life and past lives, inspiration from a higher self, messages from other persons and beings, otherworldly visions, etc., will never be complete. In the final analysis, our inner worlds seem to have far greater extent than does our "outer world" of so-called *reality*.

Yet "catalog" we must, for every variety of dream humans experience does have some form of functional value to the dreamer even though most dreamers ignore this valuable resource and presume dreams to be valueless. But, while our catalog divides dreams into major "categories," such as those that seem to be pure fantasy or those that may instead be predictive, it is vital to realize that every dream is unique and must be understood as a strictly personal experience of the dreamer. No matter that it may appear to be just like ten thousand or a hundred thousand others, the

---

1. In *Studies in Dreams* (London: George Allen & Unwin, 1921) Mary Arnold-Forster writes, "Personal experience seems often to contradict widely accepted theories of dream construction and origin; the truth being that dreams are of such infinite variety that no theory of their mechanism, even when formulated by the greatest of teachers, will adequately account for the whole of this wide field of human experience" (xxx–xxxi).

similarities may only offer helpful hints when the dreamer considers the details of his or her dream for a deeper understanding of the dream.

Just as this unique quality to each and every dream suggests that popular dream dictionaries can at most stimulate the dream analyst—the dreamer her- or himself—to explore the details for their specific application to the dream's unique psyche, so it also means all of the grand theories about dreams—by Freud, Jung, Fromm, and others—likewise must be seen only as helpful to the dreamer's personal study. But, it is necessary to remember that most of these theories were developed by therapists helping sick and disturbed people and hence do not necessarily apply in the universal manner Freud and others proclaimed.

Freud ultimately saw all dreams as "nighttime" representations of repressions, mostly sexual, that the dreamer's "daytime" conscious could not accept as his or her own. Jung, in contrast, saw dreams as mostly "archetypal" representations of universal myths rising out of the subconscious to offer the dreamer guidance to current problems by means of symbolic stories. While these ideas are relevant, the point remains that the dreamer makes the meaning of the dream pertinent to his or her own reality.

Even more important to the dreamer's ability to make dreams useful is to identify them in terms of the specific categories that will enable the dreamer to fully engage in specific forms of "dream working" for a better life. In other words, we are urging the dreamer to realize that there is as much value, or more, in what we can call nighttime work as in daytime work. Each involves a different kind and level of consciousness, each relates to different levels and dimensions of reality, and each employs different techniques when employed actively with purpose. But, together, directed with awareness and intention, they function synergistically to vastly discover new opportunities and develop new abilities for growth, advancement, and a greater life.

Perhaps no other action you can take "awakens" the sleeping powerhouse of nighttime consciousness that occupies one-third of your life as intentional dream work.

Introduction

Knowledge and power are among the major characteristics of the self-empowered individual. Discovering ways to activate these inseparable elements to generate a dynamic cycle of power in which personal growth can be enriched and potentials can be realized is among the major goals of this book.

Throughout this book, the principles and techniques related to dream power are presented within a framework that recognizes certain dream power principles as well as the importance of individual differences and preferences. A constant focus of the book is the personal development of a workable system that balances theoretical considerations with practical applications in ways that facilitate personal growth and fulfillment. The results can be profound and enduring.

The study of dream power and the mastery of programs related to it have many rewards, among them the satisfaction of gaining new knowledge and power from within. Insight gained through dream power can often be transformed into a surging force of new growth potential. Awakening of dormant functions, resolving inner conflict, activating creativity, accelerating learning, increasing self-esteem, enriching social interactions, solving personal problems, accelerating career success, and enriching the overall quality of life are only a few of the possibilities available through dream power.

Because dreams are a natural and typically spontaneous process, even sporadic efforts can yield empowering benefits. But a persistent, organized plan that recognizes the dream's underlying dynamics and processes is usually required to initiate and maximize the power of dreams. A major goal of this book is the development of a comprehensive dream power plan that is both multifaceted and multifunctional. The detailed programs presented in this book, often in step-by-step form, are each designed to promote a spiraling process that is positive and enduring. Each program recognizes the complex processes underlying dream power as well as the wide range of individual differences and preferences. The principles and techniques presented throughout the book consequently emphasize the basic characteristics of the dream-empowered state, including expanded inner awareness, increased self-esteem, positive expectations of success, and accelerated personal growth. Through dreams that interact with these essential components, both inner and outer sources of personal empowerment can become accessible and effectively activated.

Toward a Philosophy of Dream Power

Dream power is a dynamic internal process that recognizes both the inner and outer sources of knowledge, growth, and power. Often achievement oriented, it can reveal effective ways of accelerating personal growth and achieving otherwise unattainable goals. Goals related to personal relationships and careers appear particularly receptive to dream power.

As an active internal force, dream power is multifunctional in its capacity to identify barriers to success and activate effective ways of either coping with them or removing them altogether (Slate 1997). Fortunately, dream power is receptive to dreamer intervention both before sleep and during the dream experience. Goal-related suggestions presented before sleep can influence dream power to identify effective approaches in achieving them. Dream power is likewise receptive to personal intervention during sleep that, in some instances, directs the dream process toward desired results and motivates the dreamer to achieve them.

Among the major characteristics of dream power is its multifunctional capacity to motivate the dreamer by introducing new possibilities for growth and success. It can as needed connect the dreamer to higher dimensions of power, including the spiritual realm, as a source of totally new insight and power. It can, in some instances, provide solutions to personal problems and effectively ventilate the stress related to them. It can identify the subconscious sources of growth barriers and provide the enlightenment required to resolve them.

Dream power is especially receptive to goals related to personal relationships and career success. It can identify barriers and ways of removing them. It can provide enlightenment related to interpersonal conflicts, including effective ways of resolving them. It can facilitate effective decision-making by identifying options and the potential consequences of choices related to them.

The complexity of dream power is reflected in its capacity to probe the past, present, and future alike. It can retrieve relevant past experiences, probe existing realities, and interact with the future, including the afterlife dimension. The results are not only expanded awareness but personal enrichment beyond that of any other source. Dream power thus becomes an essential source of personal enlightenment, quality growth, and new power that, in some instances, is beyond that of any other source.

Dream Power Research by PRIF

Referenced throughout this book are numerous technical reports of research projects conducted under the auspices of the Parapsychology Research Institute and Foundation (PRIF), an organization established at Athens State University (ASU) in 1970 for the express purpose of promoting research and establishing student scholarships. The major focus of PRIF, now a non-college-affiliated group, remains the discovery of new knowledge and the development of effective ways to use it along with the funding of student scholarships based on financial need.

With the establishment by the author of PRIF at ASU in 1970, parapsychology rapidly became a critical component to the university's instructional and research program. Upon the introduction of parapsychology into the curriculum and the establishment of an experimental parapsychology laboratory, a variety of research efforts were implemented, including experimental projects funded by the US Army, the Parapsychology Foundation of New York, and numerous private sources. With the assistance of Dr. James E. Bathurst, a clinical psychologist and former Academic Dean of the university (then college), parapsychology gave both diversity and quality to the school's academic program. Experimental Parapsychology, Seminar in Parapsychology, and Special Topics in Parapsychology rapidly became among the university's most popular courses.

The PRIF research projects referenced in the book by technical research report (TR) number are listed in the references section at the end of the book. The reports, which exist at present in unpublished form, are on file in the ASU Library Archives and are not available for publication or distribution.

Chapter 1
Dreams: Spinners of Power

We are such stuff
As dreams are made on, and our little life
Is rounded with a sleep!
—WILLIAM SHAKESPEARE

Dreams as potential sources of enlightenment and power have intrigued cultures for centuries. Although the dream experience often occurs within a complex interactive system, there remains almost universal recognition of the relevance of dreams. It is conceivable, in fact, that nothing is more effective than the dream experience in unraveling the mysteries of our existence. A greater understanding of dream power and mastering ways of effectively using it thus become among our major challenges.

Fortunately, contemporary research has progressively increased our understanding of dreams and has dispelled many of the misconceptions related to sleep and the dream state. The following conclusions are generally supported by major dream studies, including those conducted at Athens State University under the auspices of the Parapsychology Research Institute and Foundation (TR-72):

- The typical eight-hour period of uninterrupted sleep generally consists of four or five dream periods with the duration of each period successively increasing from about ten minutes for the first period to approximately thirty to fifty minutes for the final period. As the duration of the dream period increases, the dream experience typically becomes more vivid, colorful, and easily recalled upon awakening.

- Two brief transitional stages typically characterize sleep: the *hypnagogic sleep stage* occurs between wakefulness and sleep, and the *hypnopompic sleep stage* occurs just before spontaneously awakening. Both stages are characterized by dreamlike content believed to be of little subconscious significance.

- Dreams commonly occur during *rapid eye movement* (REM) periods of sleep; however, they have been known to occur during *non-rapid eye movement* (NREM) periods as well.

- The frequency, intensity, and duration of dreams as well as the ability to recall dreams vary greatly among individuals and for the same individual over a period of time.

- Numerous factors, including environmental, physiological, and psychological, appear to influence the dream experience.

- Occasionally, the dreamer is aware of the dream as it occurs while sensing the faculties of normal consciousness, a phenomenon known as the *lucid dream*.

- Although it is believed that everyone dreams, some individuals report never having recalled a dream.

- Dreams can provide observational windows and interactive doorways to both inner and outer sources of knowledge and power.

- A specific dream can have multiple meanings and applications.

- The dream state is receptive to a variety of intervention techniques that focus on desired objectives.

Why Study Dreams?

The study of dreams is based largely on the capacity of dreams to link conscious awareness to a dynamic reserve of subconscious growth resources. Equally as important, an immense body of evidence shows the capacity of dreams to actively engage external dimensions of power. By paying attention to your dreams as purposeful states of consciousness, your dreams can become major entryways to vast new realms of enlightenment and power (TR-152).

Because of the capacity of dreams to engage both inner and outer sources of power, you can experience through your dreams totally new possibilities for growth and personal empowerment. On a very broad scale, even goals related to the complexities of our endless existence in the multiverse are receptive to recent advancements in dream power technology.

The Observational and Interactive Nature of Dream Power

Although numerous theories exist regarding the purposes of dreams, the study of dreams conducted by the author under the auspices of PRIF at Athens State University consistently showed both the observational and interactive nature of dream power (TR-72). As observational windows, dreams can provide a clear view of conditions and events relevant to the past, present, and future. Aside from that, your dreams can open a variety of interactive doorways through which you can engage the dream experience and become an active participant. Upon entering the dream's interactive doorway, you can experience the dream's capacity to engage not only your inner sources of power, but external dimensions of power as well. You can flow with your dreams and, in some instances, focus the dream action on desired outcomes through research-based intervention techniques.

It is important to note that a single dream experience is often multifunctional in its capacity to provide observational windows while opening interactive doorways. Both functions, by working together, can generate a profound increase in self-empowerment that gives new meaning to your existence.

Among the major categories of dreams as observational windows and interactive doorways to new power are:

Exploratory Dreaming: Through exploratory dreaming, which is typically spontaneous, you can effortlessly discover firsthand the multiple sources of dream power available to you at the moment. Personal enlightenment and professional advancement are both highly receptive to exploratory dreaming.

Initiative Dreaming: Through initiative dreaming, you can actively initiate specific dream experiences that focus on specific outcomes. You can balance your weaknesses, amplify your strengths, and integrate various inner potentials as sources of new power.

Interventional Dreaming: Through interventional dreaming, you can unleash and energize dormant inner potentials. You can initiate dream actions and deliberately influence dream outcomes. Through interventional dreaming, often called success dreaming, you can become empowered to achieve such personal goals as accelerating learning, improving memory, dissolving barriers, improving social relationships, and increasing motivation, to list but a few of the possibilities.

Protective Dreaming: Protective dreaming is a sleep defense mechanism that is initiated either spontaneously during sleep or deliberately through pre-sleep defense techniques designed to protect sleep from any invading negative influence.

Creative Dreaming: Through creative dreaming, also known as inventive dreaming, you can generate innovative concepts and ground-breaking solutions far beyond those previously known. Many important inventions and major advancements in science are associated with creative dreaming.

Sequential Dreaming: Through sequential dreaming, also known as serial dreaming, complex subconscious messages can be conveyed to consciousness through an interrelated sequence of dreams that can span several days or longer. They often reveal step-by-step solutions to multifaceted problem situations. By including each dream in your personal dream journal, you can dramatically increase your understanding of the relevance of the sequential dream.

Restorative Dreaming: Through restorative dreaming, you can overcome growth blockages, resolve conflicts, extinguish phobias, break disempowering habits, and strengthen relationships, to list but a few of the possibilities. Often called rejuvenative dreaming, restorative dreaming can slow the aging process and, in some instances, reverse the mental and physical effects of aging. Restorative dreaming typically reverberates throughout the dreamer's total being and is evident instantly upon awakening

Extrasensory Dreaming: Through extrasensory dreaming, you can exceed the conventional limits of perception, knowledge, and power. You can experience telepathic dreams that activate communication with others, clairvoyant dreams that generate perception of distant realities, and precognitive dreams that produce awareness of future events. Along another line, extrasensory dreaming has been known to be accompanied by psychokinetic dreaming that literally intervenes into distant physical realities in ways that bring forth positive change.

> *Caution:* It is important to note here the existence of the so-called *boomerang effect* that automatically negates any effort to use extrasensory dream power for negative purposes.

Therapeutic Dreaming: Through therapeutic dreaming, you can experience the personal therapist of highest

potential, the one existing within yourself. A single therapeutic dream experience can be worth hours of psychotherapy. Therapeutic dreaming can generate an empowered state that replaces feelings of inferiority, insecurity,
and guilt with feelings of adequacy and well-being. Venti-
lating stress, resolving conflict, overcoming growth barriers, and breaking unwanted habits, to list but a few, are all
within the scope of therapeutic dreaming.

Intradimensional Dreaming: The intradimensional dream
experience functions within the self as an essential link
between conscious and subconscious processes. Through
intradimensional dreaming, internal psychological processes become active and receptive to dream power. The
resultant interaction typically includes symbolism and
various other dream mechanisms.

Interdimensional Dreaming: Through interdimensional
dreaming, you can interact with higher dimensions of
power, including the spirit realm, and actively engage
their resources, including personal guides, guardians,
and growth specialists. Interactions with the departed
are likewise viewed by many as within the scope of interdimensional dreaming.

These are only a few of the categories of dreams as
observational windows and interactive doorways for personal growth, enlightenment, and power. When we add to

these a host of specific subclassifications, the possibilities of dream power become seemingly unlimited. Because of recent research-based advancements in dream power technology as presented in this book, you can at last discover the empowering potentials of your dreams and apply them to add new meaning and power to your life.

The Multifunctional Nature of Dream Power

The categorization of dreams as observational windows and interactive doorways recognizes the capacity of dreams to work within the framework of existing mental faculties and skills while at the same time reaching far beyond them to engage other sources of power. Because of that creative, complex nature of dreams, a single dream experience can have multiple functions. It can generate highly innovative concepts while activating a profound motivational state to apply them. The results can include far-reaching benefits of both personal and interpersonal relevance. Beyond these, dream power can be of global relevance in its far-reaching capacity to identify global problems and promote global progress (TR-72).

The many reports of dreams as important sources of both scientific and humanitarian advancements reflect the remarkable capacity of dream power to promote not only personal progress but global advancement as well. By paying attention to your dreams and seeing them as receptive states of consciousness, you can implement empowering techniques that produce profound results. *Dreamtime* thus becomes potentially as important as *daytime* at promoting personal empowerment and success.

Fortunately, you can take charge of the spontaneous dream experience while creating a totally new dream experience through dreaming intervention strategies, including pre-sleep suggestion and intervention during the dream experience.

The following are among the many areas of personal empowerment relevance available through either spontaneous dreaming or dream power intervention:

- Discovering both inner and outer sources of power
- Unleashing dormant potentials
- Promoting self-enlightenment
- Facilitating and increasing creativity
- Expanding awareness beyond known borders
- Accelerating learning
- Increasing well-being
- Addressing personal problems and concerns
- Enriching social interactions
- Amplifying strengths while balancing weaknesses

- Promoting better health, healing, fitness, and quality of life
- Slowing aging
- Improving memory
- Resolving inner conflict and insecurities
- Addressing spiritual concerns
- Promoting inner peace
- Overcoming depression
- Building self-esteem
- Eliminating barriers to personal and professional success
- Enhancing personal skills
- Promoting life-force interactions
- Transcending existing sensory borders and limitations
- Explaining the unexplainable
- Acquiring knowledge beyond known borders
- Interacting with the spiritual dimension as a source of enlightenment and power
- Exploring the unknown (including extraterrestrial life and the possible existence of other universes)
- Connecting to nature
- Discovering the bidirectional endless nature of personal existence
- Resolving conflict

Among the global areas considered relevant to dream power are the following:

- Promoting positive international interactions
- Advancing human rights
- Promoting global quality of life
- Facilitating humanitarian advancement
- Promoting world peace
- Resolving global conflict
- Protecting and enhancing the environment
- Advancing animal rights
- Promoting holistic quality of life
- Solving global economic problems—income disparity
- Addressing racism
- Addressing international environmental issues
- Addressing global healthcare issues
- Ending war and terrorism
- Eliminating pollution
- Addressing climate change
- Solving unemployment
- Ending poverty

Through dream power intervention and the resultant enlightenment, problem areas can be identified and insight related to positive solutions, including effective prevention or intervention measures, can unfold (TR-75).

These are only a few of the personal and global issues found to be receptive to dream power. Dream power in its various forms and applications is a consistently positive, empowering force. Through dream work, you can personally influence the dream experience in ways that promote both personal and global empowerment. It is important to note, however, that any intent to negatively use the power of dreams can generate the boomerang effect, in which the negative intent returns to disempower the dreamer.

Dream Work

Through the detailed approaches presented in this book, including step-by-step dream intervention techniques, you can become personally empowered to work with your dreams as they work with you (Slate 1991). Through dream work, you can discover how to open totally new corridors of power and personal growth. By working with your dreams, you can clarify your personal goals and identify ways of achieving them. From increasing self-empowerment to promoting global advancement, dream work challenges each of us to actively engage our dreams and apply their specific powers.

By working with your dreams, you can discover the relevance of such dream functions as symbolism, antithesis, and retrieval of relevant subconscious resources. You can discover the power of your dreams to both identify and activate dormant potentials related to your current goals. Overcoming growth barriers, building self-esteem, resolving subconscious barriers, and promoting powerful expectations of success are all possible through dream work that focuses on relevant subconscious functions.

Dream power can empower you to discover the relevance of manifest and latent dream content. You can discover the multiple capacities of manifest content, including protecting sleep, ensuring recall of the dream, and promoting awareness of the latent content in ways that facilitate resolution and growth. Fortunately, simply reflecting on the dream experience upon awakening and recording it in detail in your dream journal is often sufficient to facilitate enlightenment and growth related to the dream experience.

Through dream work, you can discover how to work with sequential dreams in ways that identify its relevance, including that of a current dream in the sequence. As the series of dreams unfolds, you will discover your capacity to work with the sequence in ways that influence its directions and outcomes. The sequential dream can thus become an unfolding road map to success.

Dream work can reveal the potential of your dreams to promote not only your personal empowerment but global advancement as well. Building bridges between cultures is not beyond the scope of dream power. Through dream work, you can discover the relevance of dreams concerning such diverse global issues as depletion of our natural resources, pollution of our environment, and abuse of human and animal rights, to list but a few. You can identify effective problem-solving approaches that include working with others in an effort to make the world a better place for present and future generations. Through dream work that embraces dream power, you can discover more effective ways of achieving common goals. Predictive dreaming provides a clear example of how dream power can be applied to help make the world a better place for present and future generations.

By working with your dreams, you can discover causal dreaming as among the most powerful dream experiences known. While certain dreams ask questions and expect answers, the causal dream is a three-fold problem-solving phenomenon that generates intention, provides a workable formula, and ensures success. The causal dream is applicable to an extensive range of goals. Personal growth and professional success are particularly receptive to causal dreaming. It often spontaneously focuses on evolving adversity and identifies ways to arrest it and reverse its negative effects.

Through dream work, you can discover the supreme power of dreams to actively engage the astral realm with its multiple sources of power, including spirit guides, astral growth specialists, and advanced astral planes of power. As interdimensional in nature, astral dreaming can be observational, interactive, or a combination of both. Observational astral dreaming can be a source of enlightenment through inactive observation, whereas interactive astral dreaming includes the dreamer's active participation in the unfolding experience. Through advanced dream work, the observational astral dream can intervene in ways that help shape desired outcomes.

Among the common results of astral dreaming is enlightenment related to spirituality and the astral realm. The results can include heightened awareness of the past, present, and future; increased feelings of personal worth; clarification of personal goals; resolution of personal conflicts; and a host of benefits related to health, fitness, and rejuvenation. When stated goals are included in astral dreaming, the results can be profound.

Diversity of Dream Power Programs

The numerous dream power programs presented in this book, including highly specific step-by-step procedures, are typically research-based and designed for specific applications. They are, however, often flexible and multifunctional.

Given even minor modifications, a particular program can become applicable to other dream power goals. Research consistently shows that through the repeated practice of a particular program, a positive transfer effect that accelerates the mastery of other dream power programs is often generated (TR-72).

Dream Power Readiness Program

Because dream power is a natural and often spontaneous goal-oriented process, even sporadic empowerment efforts to interact with your dreams can yield profound results. Perhaps not surprisingly, deliberately organized dream-intervention efforts related to specific goals can initiate goal-related dreams of extraordinary power. The Dream Power Readiness Program (TR-160) is designed to achieve that important goal. As a dream power program related to specifically stated goals, it can effectively generate a state of dream power readiness that facilitates relevant dreams as sources of both insight and power.

Through the program developed by PRIF, you can enhance both the relevance and effectiveness of your dreams as sources of new growth, success, and power. The program can result in dream experiences that activate the subconscious resources required to solve pressing problems, ventilate stress, resolve personal conflicts, and clarify personal goals, to list but a few of the possibilities.

This program recognizes the complex nature of dream power and its relevance to a variety of personal goals. Each step in the program is flexible and readily adaptable to individual differences in preferences and needs. In fact, dreamer intervention into the application of the plan can often increase its overall effectiveness. Here's the program, which is self-administered in a safe, secure place free of distractions either during the day or prior to sleep:

STEP 1: SPECIFY YOUR GOAL AND RECORD IT IN YOUR DREAM JOURNAL

Decide what you want to achieve and write it down. Identify the desired goal as clearly and specifically as possible. If your goal is to complete a college degree, identify a desired completion date. If your goal is to lose weight, specify the amount. If your goal is professional success, describe success in objective terms.

STEP 2: THINK VISUALLY

Visualize yourself in the process of achieving your goal or in the "goal achieved" situation. Surround yourself with positive energies of success as you imagine yourself in the future success situation.

STEP 3: DEVELOP A PLAN FOR SUCCESS

Formulate a workable, step-by-step plan that lists resources and ways of applying them to achieve your goal. Explore the interrelated relevance of your resources to your goal while identifying other required resources and ways of acquiring them. For each deficiency in resources, identify, if possible, potential remediation options and list them. Keep in mind that many unexplored and underdeveloped resources exist within you.

Step 4: Generate Commitment

The commitment process will usually consider specific questions: Why is this goal important to me at this time? What are the benefits of achieving this goal? What resources and techniques related to this goal are at present available to me?

Step 5: Maintain Motivation

By identifying and visualizing your goal, you can generate a strong motivational state required for success. The motivational state, however, is not always fixed. You can maintain a high level of motivation by recognizing the intrinsic value of personal progress associated with your goal through self-reinforcement in which you reward yourself for progress.

Step 6: Use Self-Affirmations

Recognize your progress with clear affirmations of success. If your progress is interrupted, look for ways to overcome resistance and affirm your commitment to achieve your goal. Remember that dwelling on failure is disempowering.

If one strategy fails, try another. The most powerful self-affirmation is simply *I can do it!* That simple affirmation can become a fountainhead of inner power.

STEP 7: MAINTAIN BALANCE

Balance (along with variety) is the spice of life. Keep your balance. You will find that such balancing techniques as meditation, progressive relaxation, and self-hypnosis not only facilitate your problem-solving efforts and progress in achieving goals, but they also contribute to your general well-being and self-empowerment.

STEP 8: EXERCISE VARIETY

Through the use of a variety of dream power techniques, you can build your self-confidence, generate self-fulfilling expectations of success, and supplement other self-empowering skills.

STEP 9: DEVELOP AN INTERNAL LOCUS OF CONTROL

A basic concept of dream power holds that the most important sources of power rest within yourself. Through dream power, you can develop an internal state of control. Claim ownership of your goals, and activate your plan for success now.

Step 10: Perform a Pre-sleep Review and Affirmation

In the relaxed, drowsy state prior to sleep, review your goals and reaffirm your success in achieving them. This step is usually sufficient to initiate empowering dreams related to your specifically stated goals.

———

This program is multifunctional in its capacity to generate an empowerment readiness state that is receptive to the dream experience. As a result, relevant dream power channels become readily accessible to intervention that specifically focuses them to designated goals. The program is especially effective for goals related to personal concerns related to problem-solving, decision-making, and a variety of stress-related situations. Each step in the program is flexible and readily adaptable to individual differences in preferences and needs.

Summary

Through the multifunctional power of dream work, you can experience the full scope of your existence, from the basic nature of your being to the highest levels of personal enlightenment and power. Once you are committed to developing the multifunctional power of your dreams, you are well on your way to actualizing your existing potentials while generating totally new growth possibilities.

As a consistently positive force, dream power reaches far beyond typically perceived limits. It is bidirectional in its capacity to guide you into your past and future alike. Rather than fixed, it is dynamic and interdimensional, revealing totally new realms of power and initiating empowering interactions with them. It is multiversal in its capacity to reach beyond the perceived limits of the known universe.

Fortunately, dream power with its unparalleled potentials is now available to everyone. It can empower you with the insight, self-esteem, balance, and skills required to fulfill your highest potentials. It can empower you with success in achieving otherwise unattainable goals. Through dream power, you can make success your destiny.

Chapter 2

The New Science of Dream Power

Nurture great thoughts,
for you will never go higher than your thoughts.
—BENJAMIN DISRAELI

Although spontaneous manifestations of dream power are common both during and after dreaming, the dream experience by its intrinsic nature challenges us to deliberately engage its empowering potentials and purposefully apply them. Fortunately, a dynamic new science of dream power is now emerging that empowers us to do just that. The new science progressively increases our understanding of dream power and dispels many of the misconceptions related to it. Based largely on research, including surveys, case reports, and controlled laboratory studies conducted by PRIF, dream power science recognizes the spontaneous power of dreams as well as our capacity to work with our dreams as they work with us to maximize that power.

As an emerging science, dream power steadfastly embraces a rational view that emphasizes a logical and orderly framework while recognizing diversity and individuality. It is a science that, like our own personal evolvement, is neither rigid nor automatic but instead dynamic and progressive. Through advancing our understanding of the power of our dreams, it is a science that promotes a deeper understanding of not only our dreams, but also the very nature of our existence—past, present, and future.

The Conscious, Preconscious, and Subconscious: A Dynamic, Interactive System

The new science of dream power focuses largely on a dynamic three-way interactive system that includes the conscious, preconscious, and subconscious components of our being. Consistent with psychoanalytic contributions, the conscious signifies awareness of its mental contents, including thoughts, feelings, beliefs, orientations, perceptions, and behaviors. The preconscious includes mental contents that are not present to awareness but are readily accessible. The subconscious, on the other hand, signals unawareness of a vast inner repository of knowledge, energy, and power. Rather than rigidly confined within strict controlling borders, the conscious, preconscious, and subconscious persistently interact in ways that challenge us to discover their collective powers. Together, they are the essence of our existence as evolving beings. They provide not only specific contents but a three-dimensional, interactive system that is unique to each individual (Weschcke and Slate 2009).

Rich in untapped potential, the subconscious challenges the dreamer to discover and apply its powers. Through dream power intervention, you can activate dormant subconscious powers and unleash a fresh, creative surge of new growth resources. As a result, you will discover new meaning to your existence as a being of worth whose destiny is endless growth and greatness.

Through advanced dream-power techniques, you can now reach far beyond conventionally prescribed limits to discover totally new sources of power, both within your own being and beyond. You can interact with the preconscious to directly tap into the subconscious, including its deepest levels. As a result, you can not only identify hidden potentials, but you can also unleash them to instantly empower your life. Past achievements, including mastery of complex skill, can be accessed and reactivated. Growth barriers, such as constricting phobias and obsessions, including those related to traumatic past-life experiences, can be instantly extinguished through dream power that reveals their sources, a clear example of the liberating power of knowledge.

In its capacity to reach far beyond conventionally defined borders, dream power often taps directly into external sources of power, including higher energy planes and spiritual realms. Interactions with personal guides and growth specialists through dreams are not unusual. They often occur, however, in a disguised form called *power disguiser* that promotes dreamer embracement of the interaction. Fortunately, new dream power science includes techniques specifically designed to discover higher realms of power and facilitate empowering interactions with them.

Bidirectional Endlessness of Life

Dream power science recognizes the bidirectionally endless nature of your personal existence within a four-dimensional spectrum that includes:

1. Your endless existence before your first lifetime.

2. Your existence in each lifetime.

3. Your existence between lifetimes.

4. Your endless existence after your last lifetime.

Though it may seem incomprehensible at first, only that which has no beginning has no ending. According to the bidirectionally endless view of life, your endless existence after your last lifetime must be counterbalanced by your endless existence before your first lifetime. Logically, you cannot have one without the other. Consequently, when we objectively look backward into our past, we see no beginning; and when we look forward into our future, we see no ending. Given, however, the vastness of the known universe along with the possible existence of other universe systems called the multiverse, dream power technology does not exclude the possibility that we may have existed in other realities or forms that remain at present unknown to us.

Because of recent advancements in dream power science, you can now experience retrocognitive awareness of relevant past experiences not otherwise available to conscious awareness. Complementing that, you can activate precognitive awareness of relevant future conditions and events. Not unlike the span of your personal existence, the span of dream power thus becomes endless.

Knowledge Is Power

Dream power science as an emerging body of knowledge is based largely on the concept that knowledge is power. Given the power of knowledge, it would follow that self-knowledge is self-empowering. The more you know about yourself and the nature of your existence, including your past, present, and future, the more self-empowered you become. Through scientific dream power techniques, the dream experience becomes a source of knowledge and power unlike any other source. Supportive of that view is the generally accepted concept that the more teachers know about their students, the more efficient they become in guiding student development. It would then seem only reasonable to conclude that the more we know about ourselves through dream power techniques, the more efficient we become in developing our highest potentials. As sources of personal knowledge, many dreams appear to be past-life related. They provide in many instances enlightenment concerning not only the sources of growth barriers but also ways of overcoming them. Future-life related dreams can be likewise empowering in that they can provide reassurance of our continued growth and development.

Dream Reflection and Interpretation

By reflecting on the dream experience upon awakening and promptly recording it in your dream journal, you can facilitate interpretation that clarifies the dream's purpose, including its relevance to your past, present, and future. You can determine whether the dream experience was spontaneous, or whether it was influenced by your preparation before sleep or by your intervention during dreaming.

Through reflection upon awakening, you can increase your recall of the dream, including its cognitive and affective contents. You can often identify the dream's time-related contents—including past and present—along with ways you can intervene to shape future events. By reflecting on the dream's emotional content, you can often experience its therapeutic benefits, including the ventilation of stress. Future reflections in the days and weeks following the dream, along with any spontaneous recall of the dream, can markedly increase your awareness of the dream's relevance.

Dream Intervention Techniques

Through research-based dream intervention techniques, you can influence the dream experience before, during, and after dreaming in ways that maximize its empowering effects. Through advanced pre-sleep techniques, you can influence the dream experience prior to sleep; whereas through during-sleep techniques, you can intervene into the dream experience as it occurs. Finally, through post-sleep techniques, you can apply the resultant dream power. Through mastery of these essential components of dream intervention, you can increase your understanding of the dream experience and its relevance to your existence, including past, present, and future. You can effectively activate a host of new growth possibilities, including the discovery of new knowledge and ways of applying it to enrich your life.

Dream Cycle

Dreams, it is believed, often influence our psychological state and personal adjustment, whereas our psychological state and personal adjustment often influence our dreams. Consequently, a *dream cycle* develops. A depressed psychological state often results in a depressing dream, which in turn generates an increasingly depressed post-sleep state. Likewise, a highly stressful dream can dispose the dreamer to post-sleep anxiety, which in turn generates additional stressful dreams. Fortunately, the vicious cycle can be broken and the negative influences of such dreams offset or reversed by appropriate suggestions presented in the pre-sleep state and post-sleep state.

Complexity Seeks Simplicity

Dream power science, while embracing the complexity of dreams, recognizes the familiar concept that complexity seeks simplicity. PRIF's review of personal dream journals (TR-141) showed that the simplest of dream intervention techniques were often among the most powerful. For instance, merely contemplating a problem situation during the drowsy state preceding sleep can result in dream power that provides critical insight related to the problem and ways of solving it. The success-oriented dream often generates a positive expectancy effect that increases motivation and the probability of success.

Finger-Spread Technique

Among the simplest and yet most highly effective dream intervention procedures is the research-based Finger-Spread Technique (TR-188), which is self-administered during the relaxed, drowsy state immediately preceding sleep. Here's the five-step technique, which is relevant to an extensive range of personal goals:

1. While resting comfortably in a relaxed position prior to sleep, state your goal and affirm your intent to achieve it.
2. Spread the fingers of either hand as you affirm your intent to achieve your stated goal.
3. While holding the finger-spread position, affirm your intent to work with your dreams as they work with you to achieve your stated goal.
4. Slowly relax your fingers, and as drowsiness deepens, visualize yourself succeeding in achieving your stated goal.
5. Upon awakening, note the powerful expectation of success as you affirm, *I am fully empowered to achieve my stated goal. Success is my destiny!*

The Finger-Spread Technique is especially effective when used as a problem-solving procedure. Among college students, it has been widely used to improve academic performance, clarify career goals, and promote positive social interactions. A prelaw student and member of PRIF reported having used the technique to dramatically improve her grade point average. Through her use of the technique she immediately reduced her stress level and increased her self-confidence. She became more interested in her coursework and more fully confident that she would achieve her career goal. Now a successful defense attorney, she reports that her continued use of the Finger-Spread Technique not only facilitates restful sleep and positive dreams, but it also generates a powerful expectancy effect that enriches her life and promotes success in her career (TR-188).

Summary

Through research-based concepts and techniques, dream power science can empower you to both clarify your dreams and maximize their empowering effects. Through dream work as detailed in the following chapters, you can achieve a positive state of knowledge, balance, and empowerment required to overcome growth barriers, achieve your stated goals, and facilitate the actualization of your highest potentials. Achieving that self-empowered state while contributing to the greater good is why we are here at this moment in this lifetime.

Chapter 3

The Personal Dream Journal: A Self-Empowering Venture

Explore thyself. Herein are demanded the eye and the nerve.

—HENRY DAVID THOREAU

The multifunctional nature of dreams as internal windows and doorways reflects the critical importance of keeping a personal dream journal. By reflecting on the dream experience and journaling it immediately upon awakening—especially when you are awakened by the dream—you can markedly increase the value of the dream as a source of knowledge and power. A few short notes upon awakening can be later expanded to include a more detailed entry with relevant recordings that are appropriate for later review and validation. An accurate, detailed dream journal of the personal dream experience can consequently become a powerful incentive for more advanced dream work.

Aside from satisfying the basic need to personally document the dream experience, maintaining a detailed dream journal has multiple functions (TR-141):

- It can facilitate accurate and detailed memory of dream experiences.
- It can promote understanding of the dream's relevance and underlying messages.
- It can be a valuable resource for future reference.
- It can generate insight related to recurring dreams, sequential dreams, and dreams of problem-solving relevance.
- It can increase the effectiveness of therapeutic dreams, including dreams designed to alleviate stress, resolve conflict, facilitate problem-solving, and promote career success, to list but a few.
- It can provide critical documentation for serial insight dreams that occur in stages or in logical sequences.
- It can clarify and augment the potential power of sequential, predictive, and causal dreaming.

A periodic review of the dream journal can increase its relevance, particularly for dreams of predictive and problem-solving relevance.

Personally keeping a detailed dream journal is particularly important for dreams of symbolic and extrasensory relevance, including dreams of precognitive, clairvoyant, and telepathic significance. Predictive in nature, the precognitive dream is typically designed not only to promote increased awareness of the future, but also to facilitate as needed any desired preparation or prevention of the predicted event. Future-oriented dreams can be predictive of events or conditions that range from highly positive to highly negative. As such, they can be potential sources of either disappointment or pleasurable anticipation. In competitive sports, precognitive dreaming of either winning or losing is common among athletes prior to upcoming events. According to many athletes, precognitive dreams of winning can generate a powerful *expectancy effect* that improves performance and promotes success. Recording the future-oriented dream of either winning or losing is often accompanied by heightened awareness of ways of intervening that influence outcomes and facilitate success.

The dream journal is especially important to validating dreams of clairvoyant relevance. The clairvoyant dream, for instance, is typically goal related and can hold relevance to a wide range of existing situations. The clairvoyant dream often identifies problematic conditions, along with appropriate corrective and preventive actions. Among the examples based on research by PRIF are (1) improving safety in industrial settings as the result of dreams that identify dangerous work conditions, (2) promoting the solving of crimes in law enforcement settings through clairvoyant dreams that uncover critical new evidence, and (3) eliminating health risks through clairvoyant dreams that reveal the existence of pollutants and their sources (TR-172).

A review of personal dream journals showed telepathy to be a frequent feature of the dream experience (TR-173). It can include the dream's capacity to both send and receive a wide range of messages, including communications of both cognitive and emotional relevance. It can include dream messages concerning interpersonal relations, career concerns, health issues, and leisure activities, to list but a few of the possibilities. Journaling the telepathic dream interaction tends to clarify the dream and determine its relevance.

Research by PRIF found that in times of change or transition related to careers, relationships, health, loss, and any unseen situation, keeping a dream journal can facilitate successful adaptation (TR-141).

A Functional Dream Journal Template

An effective dream journal template includes not only the essential dream elements but reflections and procedures designed to maximize the dream's empowering potentials. The following listing of elements considered essential to a functional dream power template was provided by the late Carl Llewellyn Weschcke of Llewellyn Worldwide:

Personal Data: Your name, date of birth, location, and other relevant information to include, if preferred, such as personal horoscope information.

Current Conditions: Present situations or conditions that could influence the dream experience.

The Dream Experience: Describe in detail the dream experience and your mental, emotional, and physical reactions to it. Did you awaken suddenly or naturally? If suddenly, note any words, images, or feelings that seemed to be factors in the waking process. Detail your responses to the dream, including surprise or confusion, desire to awaken and share with your partner if present, and other elements, such as the realization that it was only a dream.

Dream Origin: Describe your immediate thoughts about the origin of the dream, such as current events and concerns. Identify any obvious symbolic elements such as the surprise appearances of animals, long-forgotten people, or very strange images. Note your feelings in relation to these dream elements.

Dream Review: The following evening before sleep, take time to conduct the following three-step review of the previous night's dream. This review process, though usually brief, may take practice to develop. Again, you are switching gears and engaging a meditative process that may require several sessions to develop.

1. Look again at your notes and give particular attention to what you may now recognize as prime symbolic elements.

2. Close your eyes and briefly relax, breathing rhythmically and a little more deeply than usual. Visualize the individual symbolic elements and ask each element to complete its message to you.

3. When done, open your eyes and enter the message in your dream journal.

Periodic Review: Periodically review your recent dream journal notes and reflect upon them. Look for any evidence of *serial insight* or *sequential dreams* and their present and future relevance. Consider the deeper and larger messages of your dreams, including their relevance to your whole being—past, present, and future.

Long Term Follow-Up: At any time you recall the message of a past dream in relation to a current situation or event, record the experience in your dream journal. Note your sense of gratitude for the positive value of your dreams.

Summary

There is something about the process of recording your dreams in a personal journal that facilitates introspection and dream analysis. Keeping a dream journal can increase the immediate benefits of the dream experience along with its long-term empowering effects. The dream journal thus becomes an essential component of dream power technology.

Chapter 4

The Transcendent Dream Element: A Channel of Power

Be thine own palace, or the world's thy jail.

—JOHN DONNE

The transcendent dream element is a little-known but dynamic, interactive component of dream power. Although it is often spontaneous in promoting purposeful dream interactions, the element as a channel of dream power is receptive to deliberate intervention designed to focus the dream experience upon designated personal goals. Once activated, the transcendent dream element becomes a positive channel of power that literally elevates the dream experience to new levels of relevance, clarity, and power.

As the essential force underlying dream power, the transcendent dream element embraces the concept that self-enlightenment is self-empowering. Multifunctional in nature, the transcendent dream element can become a seismic inner force that activates the highest functions of dream power (TR-121). The results are typically threefold: (1) enlightenment concerning the subconscious sources of personal growth and power, (2) the detection of growth blockages and ways of dissolving them, and (3) the unleashing of totally new growth possibilities. Self-empowerment through the transcendent dream element is especially effective in overcoming specific growth barriers such as phobias, emotional conflicts, and feelings of insecurity. It can rapidly accelerate progress toward achieving goals related to self-enlightenment, personal well-being, health and fitness, rejuvenation, and quality of life.

There exists an evolving body of evidence showing the capacity of the transcendent dream element to generate a powerful expectancy effect that often clarifies personal goals and increases the probability of achieving them. Here are a few other examples of the empowering possibilities of the transcendent dream element as an interactive component of dream power:

- It can provide insight required for resolving personal conflicts, overcoming growth blockages, and improving social relationships.

- It can increase feelings of security and personal worth.

- It can facilitate clarification of career goals and identify ways of achieving them.

- In the academic setting, it can increase motivation, accelerate the rate of learning, and improve retention of material learned.

- It can promote enlightenment related to higher dimensions of power, including the spirit realm.

- It can retrieve relevant past experiences, including those of past-life origin.

- It can promote awareness concerning both present and future realities.

Fortunately, research-based dream empowerment programs are now available to engage the transcendent dream element and focus its interactive power on designated personal goals, from broadly general to highly specific.

Becoming Your Own Palace of Power

Through your interactions with the transcendent dream element, you can become your own palace of power. Although the transcendent dream element is often spontaneously manifested, it is receptive to dream work that focuses it on specifically designated goals, such as expanding awareness, accessing the highest sources of knowledge, dissolving growth barriers, and accelerating personal growth. At its peak, the activated element can empower you to discover the endless scope of your existence while adding new meaning to your life.

The transcendent dream element often reveals future events including the consequences of current conditions and actions. It can synthesize cognitive elements and process them in ways that increase awareness of the future, including events that are either destined or highly probable. *Destiny enlightenment* can be empowering primarily in that it can facilitate effective preparation for the future, whereas *probability enlightenment* can suggest ways of not only preparing for the future but also intervening to shape the future as needed. Together, both destiny and probability enlightenment through the transcendent dream element can be empowering in that they increase knowledge of future relevance and ways of applying it.

Transcendent Dream Activation Procedure (TDAP)

Among the most effective programs designed to engage the transcendent dream element as a channel of power is a step-by-step procedure called simply the Transcendent Dream Activation Program (TR-134). The research-based procedure recognizes the wide-ranging individual differences in the functions of the transcendent dream element. A consistent feature of that dream element, however, was found to be its receptiveness to pre-sleep intervention that included colorful imagery.

A particularly bright color, when deliberately introduced into the dream experience through pre-sleep imagery, was found to influence dream functions in ways that conveyed specific messages commonly associated with that color. The empowering relevance of a specific color was found to be consistent with that of colors found in the human aura system enveloping the physical body. Here are a few examples:

- Dreams with **green** coloration are associated with positive mental and physical functions related to better quality of life. Bright green is associated with health, fitness, rejuvenation, and longevity.

- **Yellow** is associated with positive social relationships, higher intelligence, and social skills. When deliberately introduced into dreams, bright yellow can facilitate success in achieving a wide range of personal goals.

- **Bright blue** is associated with tranquility, cheerfulness, and optimism. Dreams of bright blue coloration often generate a positive mood state while predicting desirable outcomes.

- Dreams with **red** coloration, including flashes of bright red, signify unexpected challenges and emergency situations. The need for caution is signaled by dreams of red.

- **Purple** is typically associated with artistic potential, spiritual enlightenment, and humanitarian concerns, including issues such as injustice, prejudice, and discrimination.

- **Brown** is associated with practicality and the importance of rational decision-making.

- **Orange** is associated with positive social interactions, assertiveness, and persuasive skills.

- **Pink** is associated with sensitivity and idealism.

- Dreams with shades of **gray** are associated with practicality, reason, and in some instances, skepticism.

The Transcendent Dream Activation Program is an easily implemented step-by-step procedure that focuses dream power on a wide range of designated goals. Although typically implemented during the drowsy state preceding sleep, the procedure, with minor revisions, can be effectively implemented under other conditions, including a variety of meditation and relaxation approaches. Here's the procedure:

Step 1: Goal Statement

Formulate your goal and affirm your commitment to achieve it.

Step 2: Color Selection

Mentally select a color related to your goal statement. For instance, if your goal is to enrich intellectual functions, the preferred color is bright yellow. On the other hand, if your goal is to promote health and fitness, the preferred color is bright green.

Step 3: Pre-sleep Relaxation and Affirmation

While resting comfortably in a reclining position, relax your full body by mentally scanning it from your forehead downward while affirming, *I am now becoming more and more relaxed.* Take as much time as needed to relax your full body.

Step 4: Color Visualization

As drowsiness ensues, visualize the previously selected color as a channel of energy connecting you to the inner Dream X Element as a central part of your being.

Step 5: Affirmation

Affirm, *As I sleep, I will be receptive to dream power related to my stated goal. I will have full recall of the dream experience, and I will be fully empowered to achieve my goal.*

Step 6: Post-sleep Reflection

Upon awakening, reflect on the dream experience and note its empowering effects. Again, affirm your success in achieving your stated goal.

————

The post-sleep results of dream color intervention are often prompt and profound. The therapeutic effects of bright colors are especially effective for stress and mood-related disorders. Dreams with bright color content were also found to be effective in unleashing a variety of creative functions and promoting awareness of unexpected future events, particularly those related to unusually bright coloration in the dream experience.

The effects of color intervention often include post-sleep changes in the individual's aura, the energy system enveloping the physical body. Included was a temporary expansion of the full aura as well as increased brilliance in aura color. In instances of health-related concerns, clusters of bright green signaling healing energy often become visible in the aura at the relevant body area (Slate 1999).

The Problem-Solving Power of the Transcendent Dream Element

Problem-solving power is a common but complex component of the transcendent dream element (TR-133). It can diagnose the problem and identify the dynamics related to it, including its causes and effects. It can identify alternative solutions and highlight the preferred one. It can specifically access the relevant subconscious problem-solving resources and convey them to consciousness. Here are a few examples of the problem-solving power of the transcendent dream element:

Career Decisions: The transcendent dream element can identify the essential factors related to career decisions, including those involving career preparation, future demands, and job satisfaction.

Financial Management Decisions: Through its precognitive capacities, the transcendent dream element can be a source of insight related to financial investment and management decisions.

Social Relations: Through its interactive social component, the transcendent dream element can promote positive social interactions and facilitate the resolution of social conflicts.

Although often spontaneously activated, the problem-solving component of the transcendent dream element can be implemented through a variety of pre-sleep dream intervention techniques (TR-132). Among the most effective is simply contemplating the problem during the drowsy state preceding sleep and mentally affirming that the problem-solving power of transcendent dreaming will be activated as you sleep.

The Intellectual Power
of the Transcendent Dream Element

Pre-sleep imagery of problem situations with yellow coloration is associated with highly productive dreaming that literally increases the power of the transcendent dream element to promote success in achieving challenging intellectual goals (TR-132). That possibility was illustrated by a graduate student whose pursuit of a master's degree in counseling required efficiency in advanced statistics, a requirement that evoked considerable anxiety. For several days prior to the qualifying exam, he used pre-sleep suggestions of success accompanied by bright yellow imagery to signify intellectual power. By his own report, he experienced during his exam sensations that he described as "bright yellow energy" enveloping his full body. He passed the exam with a glowing rating of excellent.

Ongoing research by PRIF provides strong evidence that practice in pre-sleep imagery of bright yellow can literally increase the level of both verbal and performance intelligence as measured by standardized tests (TR-132). Other instances of the intellectual power of the transcendent dream element include overcoming mental blockages, increasing motivation, and building a positive expectancy effect.

The Health-Related Benefits of the Transcendent Dream Element

The study of dreams by PRIF revealed a variety of health-related benefits of the transcendent dream element (TR-136). Pre-sleep relaxing imagery of a nature scene with bright green coloration, preferably iridescent, tended to activate dreams that ventilated stress and promoted a positive post-sleep mood state conducive to wellness. ASU athletes who practiced pre-sleep imagery of bright green coloration reported a marked reduction in stress along with increased self-confidence. The results often included a powerful *self-fulfilling expectancy effect* that, from their perspective, promoted self-confidence and a more optimistic outlook.

The rejuvenating effects of the transcendent dream element are often reported by older adults who regularly practice the program (TR-137). In a study conducted by PRIF, interviews with men and women who consistently practiced positive pre-sleep imagery of green following their participation in a PRIF rejuvenation seminar at ASU reported a powerful rejuvenating effect that included an increase in healthful energy as well as positive changes in physical appearance. Typically, the more specific the imagery, the more dramatic the reported rejuvenating effects. For instance, images of facial wrinkles "dissolving away" seemed to be far more effective than pre-sleep suggestions that did not include related imagery. Furthermore, the introduction of relevant coloration seemed to markedly accelerate the rejuvenation effects. The so-called technicolor dream appeared to not only generate rejuvenation, but it added quality to life as well.

The Transcendent Dream Therapist

An essential component of dream power is its therapeutic potential. PRIF research investigating the transcendent dream element often revealed therapeutic effects that appeared to reach far beyond conventional approaches (TR-138). In many instances, the transcendent dream element seems to connect the dreamer to the transcendent therapist existing within the self. Through that inner therapist whose major tool is enlightenment, increased awareness of the subconscious sources of anxiety, fixations, obsessions, compulsions, insecurity, and fear, and so on often occurs. Not infrequently, a therapeutic glimpse into the subconscious source seems not only to alleviate growth blockage but also to activate totally new growth potentials. Given enlightenment concerning the source, the positive results are often spontaneous and profound.

Phobias and conflicts related to trauma seem to be particularly receptive to therapeutic dream power that interacts with the transcendent dream element. The therapeutic role of that interaction was illustrated by the dream experience of a business executive whose fear of heights, closed spaces, and darkness had hounded him for years and persistently limited his daily activities. By his report, his participation in business-related activities was limited to those conducted in a spacious and well-lit setting at ground-floor level. Travel by air was avoided as well as ground travel that involved arching bridges or mountains. Simply viewing a mountain from a distance generated anxiety. The resultant constriction of daily life activities only added to the severity of his persistent fears. Finally, the three fears were, by his own report, fully extinguished by the therapeutic intervention of transcendent dream power that enlightened him concerning their interconnected source—an apparent past-life experience in which, as a mountain climber, he fell to his death. By his report, upon nearing the top of a snow-covered mountain, he suddenly slipped and fell into a deep snow-filled crevice. Fully buried in the snow, his struggle to free himself only sank him deeper into the dark snow-filled crevice. Upon suddenly awakening from the dream, he reportedly experienced a complete release of his fear of heights, enclosed spaces, and darkness. The enlightening result of the transcendent dream appeared not only to explain the source of the three fears but also to effectively extinguish them. Free at last from the three phobias, his life took on new meaning and his business flourished. Somewhat surprisingly, he soon developed a special interest in mountain climbing, snow skiing, and exploring dark caverns, each of which enriched his life with, in his words, "the pleasure of self-discovery" (TR-138).

The transcendent dream therapist, aside from its internal functions, seems often to reach far beyond the wealth of internal therapeutic resources to engage higher sources of therapeutic enlightenment and power. Therapeutic interactions with higher dimensions and personal spirit guides are apparently not unusual.

The Transcendent Stream of Dream Power Program

Dream power and self-empowerment are together a multifunctional force with components that interact with each other. The Transcendent Stream of Dream Power Program (TR-120) is a spoken exercise that includes two critical components of dreams power: imagery and motion. When practiced preceding sleep, it becomes multifunctional in its capacity to alleviate stress and promote relaxation. In its use of imagery and motion, it can exercise visualization, stimulate creativity, expand conscious awareness, and promote positive mind, body, and spirit interactions.

Although designed for use during the pre-sleep state, the self-empowerment program as follows can be practiced while resting comfortably under other secure conditions that are free from interruption.

The Transcendent Stream of Dream Power

I am the stream of dream power. Emerging from deep, mysterious caverns, I am slowly flowing forward into the light of awareness and experience. Patiently yet persistently, I advance toward the vast sea of understanding and expanded cosmic consciousness. At times tranquil and serene, I am momentarily content in my limited scope of knowledge; at other times I am urgent and intense, demanding to increase my knowledge and to magnify my range of conscious experience.

I am the stream of dream power. Settling into deep blue pools of introspection, languishing to reflect in the shade, I gather my resources before once again pressing forward even more vigorously, exploring, searching, discovering my inner being and the universe, forcefully unblocking barriers to my progress and growth.

I am the stream of dream power. Slowly flowing among the towering trees of aspiration and weaving among boulders of inner strength, I am cleansed, empowered, and invigorated by the positive energies and forcefulness of the universe and my own existence.

I am the stream of dream power. Flowing into a sunlit valley of peaceful contentment, I am calm, confident, and secure as I advance steadily to join the illimitable sea of universal consciousness and cosmic oneness.

———

When this program is practiced during the pre-sleep state, relevant goal-related dreams frequently emerge, often in highly vivid form. The resultant dreams are typically colorful and characterized by motion. Through improved visualization skills and expanded consciousness resulting from the practice of this exercise, the self-empowerment process is rapidly advanced and the potential for future empowerment is strengthened.

This program embraces personal existence as both endless and bidirectional. As a stream, it reaches into the endless past and extends into the endless future. Given no beginning and no end, our personal existence would seem likewise to be characterized by endless dream power.

Summary

The transcendent dream element is a dynamic force that can elevate dream power to its highest level. Consistently enlightening and empowering in nature, it can function spontaneously or it can be deliberately activated through procedures developed in the research lab setting. As an essential component of dream power, it can have a seismic multidimensional effect that empowers you to become your own palace of power.

Chapter 5
Sleep, Dreams, and Out-of-Body Experiences

The eternal mystery of the world is its comprehensibility.
—ALBERT EINSTEIN

The out-of-body relevance of sleep is based on recognition of the *astral body* and the existence of the *astral plane*. From the out-of-body perspective, sleep is often seen as a naturally occurring out-of-body state in which the astral body is spontaneously projected outside the physical body for the duration of sleep. In that projected state, the astral body remains in close proximity to the physical body except during out-of-body travel to other realities or dimensions.

As the non-biological double of the physical body, the astral body is typically associated with the spiritual nature of our being. From that perspective, the astral body is manifested by an aura of energy enveloping the physical body and related to a wide range of out-of-body experiences (OBEs), including astral travel, in which the astral body is projected beyond the biological body to experience other realities, either physical or spiritual, while remaining linked to the biological body by an energy connection commonly called the *silver cord* (Weschcke and Slate 2012).

Out-of-body experiences during sleep, while unlike dreams in dynamics, are often experienced as highly similar to vivid dreams. Whether occurring during sleep or independent of sleep, OBEs like the dream experience can result in a profound increase in both awareness and power. Differentiating OBEs from dream experiences, however, can be a difficult needle to thread. Fortunately, simply recording the experience in your dream journal can promote clarification of the experience and its relevance.

Research conducted by PRIF, including interviews with volunteer subjects, found that the reported frequency of out-of-body travel during sleep varied widely among participants in the study (TR-98). The reported frequency of spontaneous OBEs during sleep ranged from almost nightly to infrequent or uncertain. Numerous participants reported recurrent out-of-body travel to distant destinations and interactions with other out-of-body travelers. Travel to what seemed to be other dimensions, including the spirit realm and interactions with spirit beings, including personal guides, was not unusual.

Non-sleep Out-of-Body Travel

In an effort to develop an effective goal-oriented program for out-of-body travel during sleep, PRIF reviewed the non-sleep induction techniques used by 15 volunteer college students, all of whom reported having developed an effective non-sleep procedure for traveling out-of-body at will (TR-101). Participants in this survey study were 9 males and 6 females with an age range of 19 through 28 years. Following is a summary of the results:

- The physical state most conducive to out-of-body travel was characterized by progressive relaxation and drowsiness in which bodily processes (breathing and pulse rate particularly) were slowed.

- The mental state most conducive to OBEs was characterized by tranquility and motivation. A clear intent to travel out-of-body was formulated.

- Although the participants of this study often used autosuggestion, similar to hypnosuggestion, the out-of-body state was seen by all participants as clearly unlike the hypnotic state. The autosuggestions varied but typically included those similar to the following: "I am now deeply relaxed and ready to leave my body. I am free to go wherever I wish. I am in full control as I slip out of my body. I will be safe and secure throughout this experience. I will return with ease to re-engage my body when I decide to do so. I am now floating away, drifting aloft, leaving my body behind."

- For specific destination travel, images of the destination were formed by the participants and integrated into the induction phase.

- Having developed an effective non-sleep procedure for inducing the out-of-body experience, the participants of this study reported a spontaneous increase in meaningful out-of-body travel during sleep.

Based largely on these interview results related to astral travel by experienced subjects during the non-sleep state, the following procedure was developed to promote empowering out-of-body travel during sleep, which is generally considered conducive to out-of-body travel.

Astral Travel During Sleep

Astral Travel During Sleep is a step-by-step program designed to promote intentional, goal-oriented out-of-body travel during sleep (TR-102). The procedure consists of the following five stages:

Step 1: State of Intent

Before falling asleep, a clear intention to experience out-of-body travel is formulated. This pre-sleep intent state provides the motivation required to engage productive out-of-body travel. Goals, both specific and general, can be presented, and the destination for travel can be specified or left open.

Step 2: Pre-sleep Autosuggestion

As drowsiness ensues, suggestions designed to promote productive out-of-body travel are presented positively. Examples: *Upon entering sleep, I will become empowered to leave my body and travel wherever I wish. I will be safe and in full control as I travel outside my body. I will return to my body either spontaneously or at any moment I decide to do so.*

Step 3: Destination Control Imagery

For specific destination travel, a detailed mental image of the destination is formulated. For non-specific destination travel, a state of cognitive passivity is allowed to spontaneously emerge.

Step 4: Spontaneous Imagery-Astral Fusion

As drowsiness deepens and sleep ensues, sense the spontaneous imagery-astral fusion in which you become liberated to travel beyond your physical body.

Step 5: Out-of-Body Travel

To engage travel, affirm, *I am now empowered to travel out of body.*

Step 6: The Return

Following travel, the return and reengagement of your physical body at rest is either spontaneous or by simple intent and affirmation: *I am now empowered to return to my physical body and reengage it.*

———

Research by PRIF found that repeated practice of this program typically resulted in a dramatic increase in out-of-body travel during sleep as well as greater control of the experience (TR-98). The resultant astral experiences included discovery of distant realities, along with increased awareness of present and future relevance. Interactions with personal spirit guides and higher planes as sources of power dramatically increased with repeated practice of this program.

Advanced Astral Flow Program

The Advanced Astral Flow Program is a seven-step advanced procedure designed by PRIF to facilitate astral travel during sleep and to directly engage external dimensions of advanced power (TR-103). Here's the procedure:

Step 1: Preparation

In the drowsy state preceding sleep, relax your total body by mentally scanning it from your forehead downward as you release all tension. Upon completing the scan, suggest to yourself that time is slowing down.

Step 2: Affirmation
Affirm that, as you enter sleep, you will slip gently out of your body and, while remaining safe and secure, travel out-of-body to other dimensions of knowledge and power, should you decide to do so.

Step 3: Consciousness Rising
As drowsiness deepens, sense astral consciousness as a brilliant body of energy rising gently from your physical body while securely remaining connected to it by a bright cord of astral energy. Allow plenty of time for the experience to unfold as you sense your oneness with it.

Step 4: Astral Freedom
As the out-of-body state of awareness unfolds, note your sense of freedom from all physical constrictions as you rise gently upward and away from your physical body.

Step 5: Astral Flow
With the bright cord of energy remaining intact, you can flow with the experience to engage, either spontaneously or by intent, distant sources of power, including the spirit realm.

Step 6: Physical Reengagement

Although the astral flow experience typically concludes spontaneously with the reengagement of the physical body either during sleep or upon awakening, it can be ended deliberately by the simple intent to return and reunite with the physical body.

Step 7: Journal Entry

Record the experience in your dream journal.

———

In poststudy interviews, participants who practiced this research-based program reported a dramatic increase in the frequency of lucid dreaming, a phenomenon they believed could signify not only astral travel during sleep but the possibility of clairvoyant dreaming as well—yet another difficult needle to thread!

Dreams as Fusion Vehicles for OBEs

Among the most complex functions of dreams is the active fusion of dream power with the out-of-body experience (TR-98). As subconscious energizing vehicles, dreams can motivate astral travel and, in some instances, literally direct it to distant destinations, including higher planes of power. The results include interactions with personal growth specialists that function as messengers, problem-solvers, tension releasers, motivators, and growth stabilizers, to list but a few. Through the fusion of dream power and the out-of-body experience, a powerful, creative force can emerge that opens totally new corridors for conscious awareness and pushes back the limiting borders of human experience.

Paradoxically, the complex functions of dreams as astral fusion vehicles can often be activated by a simple pre-sleep suggestion: *As I sleep, dream power will activate astral power to energize me with complete success in achieving my personal goals.* As drowsiness deepens, you can increase the effectiveness of the suggestion by visualizing specific goals as evolving realities. Goals related to rejuvenation, longevity, and health along with academic and career success are particularly receptive to this program.

A journalist reported that while on a business trip, she experienced a dream that offered, in her opinion, clear evidence of dreams as fusion vehicles for out-of-body experiences (TR-102). In the dream, she visited her office and noticed that a framed picture had fallen to the floor from its location on the wall. She retrieved the picture and upon returning it to its previous location on the wall, noticed a small crack in the glass at the frame's lower left corner. Upon awakening and reflecting on the experience, she questioned whether it was a dream or an out-of-body experience.

Upon returning to her office, she examined the picture at its familiar location on the wall and noticed the small crack at the lower left corner of the glass. She again questioned whether it was a dream or an out-of-body experience. Although she concluded it was probably a combination of both, she wondered whether there were other more reasonable explanations for the unusual experience.

Out-of-Body Interactive Embracement

Research conducted by PRIF found that interactive out-of-body experiences between partners can often be effective in resolving a host of partner conflicts and promoting positive partner interactions (TR-104). When deliberately used by couples in a relationship, the out-of-body technique called out-of-body interactive embracement is jointly initiated by partners during the drowsy state between wakefulness and sleep with the express intent of mutual astral body embracement. As a pre-sleep out-of-body interactive technique, it is designed to induce empowering OBEs as well as quality sleep and productive dreaming. Out-of-body embracement has shown outstanding success in enriching partner interactions and resolving a variety of couples' issues, including psychosexual concerns. Here is the procedure:

Step 1: Orientation
Review with your partner the full procedure designed to empower couples' relationships.

Step 2: Palm-Against-Palm Contact

During the drowsy state preceding sleep, gently rest the palm of either hand against the palm of your partner's hand as you together state your intent to engage in out-of-body embracement as sleep ensues.

Step 3: Palm-Against-Palm Finger Spread

With the palm of your hand resting against that of your partner, together slowly spread your fingers and briefly hold the palm-against-palm spread position. Together with your partner, slowly relax the spread position as you become increasingly relaxed and drowsy.

Step 4: Affirmation

While remaining deeply relaxed, affirm that as you now enter sleep, you will together with your partner experience the mutual out-of-body state during which your astral body with that of your partner gently rises to become suspended above the physical body.

Step 5: Out-of-Body Embracement

Upon entering the out-of-body state, engage in out-of-body embracement in which your astral body embraces the astral body of your partner.

Step 6: Astral Interaction
During embracement, jointly engage in mutual astral interactions with your partner.

Step 7: Quality Sleep and Dreaming
Allow the astral interaction with your partner to spontaneously conclude, whereupon quality sleep and dreaming unfolds.

Step 8: Conclusion
Upon awakening, review the experience with your partner and record it in your personal dream journal.

———

Out-of-body interactive embracement has shown remarkable success when used by couples to resolve issues related to conflicts, compatibility, financial concerns, career decisions, and social interactions, to list but a few. As one couple put it, "Out-of-body interactive embracement proved far more effective than hours of psychotherapy."

Distance Partner Interaction

Research by PRIF found that partners separated by geographical distance often due to career demands frequently experience mutually meaningful interactions during sleep. Distance Partner Interaction (TR-105), a step-by-step program developed by PRIF, is specifically designed to promote positive partner interactions when practiced concurrently by couples separated by geographical distance. Whether seen as a positive dream interaction technique, an out-of-body procedure, or simply a product of creative imagination, Distance Partner Interaction has been highly effective in strengthening relationships between partners, even in situations involving long-term separation. Here's the procedure:

Step 1: Plan Overview
Together with your partner, review the full interactive procedure as follows. Mutually identify the desired setting and preferred time to implement the planned interaction.

Step 2: Pre-sleep Body Scan
While resting comfortably in a pre-sleep reclining position, take in a few deep breaths, exhaling slowly. Mentally scan your body from your forehead downward, pausing at areas of tension while affirming: *I am becoming more and more relaxed. I am becoming drowsier and drowsier.*

Step 3: Astral Awareness
As drowsiness ensues, sense the liberation of your astral being in conscious energy form slowly disengaging your physical body while remaining connected to it by an astral

energy cord. Remind yourself that your astral being, once projected, knows no physical distance limitation.

Step 4: Astral Liberation
Now liberated from the restraints of physiology, you are empowered to experience the astral presence of your partner.

Step 5: Engagement and Interaction
You are now empowered to engage in positive partner interactions, including energy embracement and interaction.

Step 6: Disengagement and Return
To conclude the out-of-body interaction with your partner, turn your attention to your physical body at rest and gently re-engage it.

Step 7: Pre-sleep Reflection
Reflect on the out-of-body interactions as drowsiness deepens and sleep ensues.

Step 8: Conclusion
Upon awakening, again reflect upon the experience along with any dreams related to it, and record them in your dream journal.

———

The Distance Partner Interaction program has been widely used by couples in a variety of settings, including the military, in which partners separated by distance routinely practiced the procedure at designated locations and times during which they experience the astral presence of their partner. Although this procedure may require considerable practice to be effective, it has shown remarkable success, not only in the couples' sustaining a positive relationship but progressively improving it even in instances of long-term separation. A US Army officer separated from his wife while serving overseas claims that regular practice of the Distance Partner Interaction procedure not only saved his marriage, but it strengthened it beyond measure. His wife, a university administrator, agreed!

Summary

The astral plane is a place of power available to everyone. Through dream power, you can personally experience it as a dimension of power unlike that of any other. Through your out-of-body interactions with it, you can discover the missing link between limited physical existence in the world and your destiny for infinite growth and permanence in the cosmos. You can experience interactions with totally new higher dimensions of power and personal growth guides that give new meaning to your existence.

Chapter 6

Symbolism: The Language of Dream Power

Life, like a dome of many-colored glass,
Stains the white radiance of Eternity.

—PERCY BYSSHE SHELLY

Among the most important goals of dream work is a more complete understanding of the dynamics, processes, and applications of the dream experience. Since symbols are used so extensively among cultures to convey meaningful messages of religious, political, and social significance, it is not surprising to find that symbolism is an essential component of dream power. The universal application of symbols, many of which have cross-cultural similarities as seen in art and communication, may be a reflection of our innate tendency to utilize symbolism in dreams to actively convey in manifest or surface form the dream's underlying content. Although the dream experience can include direct, nonsymbolic content, a recognition of symbolism as the language of dream power is essential to the understanding of dreams as positive sources of knowledge and personal empowerment (Slate 1988).

Dream symbolism in its various forms is consistently multifunctional. It protects the dreamer from the direct invasion of repressed experiences buried in the subconscious, it safeguards sleep and conveys vast quantities of information in a nonthreatening manner, it promotes retention of the dream experience, and, finally, it challenges the dreamer to discover the dream's true significance. While complicating dream analysis, symbolism reduces resistances to the dream message and prepares the dreamer for new insight and growth. It motivates and facilitates appropriate positive action once the dream message is fully understood. Having invested our energies in discovering the relevance of our dreams, we are typically far more likely to value the resultant insight and to act positively on it. Clearly, the subconscious self as teacher and dream symbols as instructional mechanisms compare favorably with the most advanced educational resources known.

A. The Intradimensional Dream:
An empowerment interaction with the self

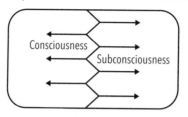

Consciousness

Subconsciousness

B. The Interdimensional Dream:
An empowerment interaction
with a dimension external to the self

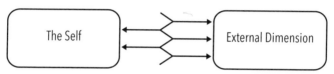

The Self

External Dimension

Intradimensional versus Interdimensional Dream Power

Both intradimensional and interdimensional dreams typically include symbolism along with other disguises, all of which are purposeful in nature. When experienced intradimensionally, the dream functions as an internal psychological process between conscious and subconscious elements. When experienced interdimensionally, the dream becomes an interactive link to external dimensions of knowledge and power. Both categories recognize dreams as sources of personal growth and empowerment. In the intradimensional dream experience, inner sources of enlightenment and power are accessed and conveyed, though often indirectly or in disguised form, to conscious awareness. In the interdimensional dream, external dimensions also as sources of enlightenment and power are accessed and conveyed to consciousness. An analysis of dream reports by PRIF revealed that, while the typical dream appears to be intradimensional in nature, the interdimensional dream is not rare and may occur with far greater frequency than commonly realized (TR-141). It is important to note that dream power in whatever form typically includes symbolism as well as other communication techniques.

Functional Dream Symbolism

Functional dream symbolism can generate an interpretation challenge while at the same time initiating a positive receptive effect (TR-72). Once the message of the dream is understood, the mission of the dream as a communication channel is fulfilled. Given the resultant insight and power, dormant subconscious resources are activated, and otherwise unattainable goals become reasonable possibilities.

The empowering potential of dream symbolism was illustrated by a college student whose infrequent but vivid dream of wild horses consistently occurred shortly before personally stressful situations. Upon recognizing the dream's predictive significance, she became increasingly effective in managing stressful situations and in some instances, fully preventing them. For her, the recurring dream became like a spiritual guide that helped build feelings of self-confidence and security (TR-171).

Symbolism in dreams is often bifunctional in its capacity to identify not only barriers to personal growth but also effective ways of overcoming them. That bifunctional role of symbolism in dreams was dramatically indicated by a college student who experienced a highly vivid intradimensional dream of a caged lion pacing restlessly back and forth. Upon awakening from the dream and reflecting on its relevance, he immediately connected it to his long-term feelings of social isolation. By his own admission, his history of social interactions revealed an impulsive and somewhat aggressive side of his personality that often resulted in interpersonal conflicts and broken relationships. Upon recording the dream and contemplating its relevance, he came to the threefold conclusion: (1) the lion represented his overly-aggressive tendencies, (2) the cage represented certain self-imposed social constrictions, and (3) the pacing behavior of the lion represented his social instability and discontent. As a result of the three-fold message of the dream and its motivational effects, his social interests rapidly increased, and he became an active participant in a variety of campus social activities. To improve his social interactions, he assumed greater control of his aggressive impulses through expanding his "caged" interests and activities into a wider range of more balanced interactions. His dream experience, which possessed both intradimensional and interdimensional elements, effectively diagnosed the condition, identified contributing factors, and prescribed corrective strategies, all in symbolic form. As the result of a single dream experience, his social life became increasingly stable and rewarding. In his senior year, he was elected president of his graduating class (TR-72).

Symbolism in dreams can convey important messages of past, present, and future relevance. While often protecting sleep through symbols that disguise potentially disturbing messages, symbolism can effectively minimize resistance to the dream message, motivate interpretation, enhance retention, and increase the overall effectiveness of the communication. Consequently, a relevant dream message conveyed symbolically and clearly understood is seldom rejected. Determining the dream's symbolic significance, however, is not always easy. As previously noted, simply reflecting upon the dream and recording the dream experience in your dream journal often results in a clearer understanding of the dream's message and its relevance. Discovering the full relevance of the dream, however, is often a slowly evolving process.

The empowering potential of dreams can be markedly increased when they include multiple interactive symbols that include a combination of interrelated symbols, such as objects, actions, and settings that possess interrelated symbolic significance (TR-72). For instance, the dream of a distant sinking ship includes action (sinking), object (ship), and setting (distant) with the possibility that the action signifies loss, the object signifies opportunity, and distance symbolizes time. A sinking ship at a great distance could, consequently, represent lost opportunity in the distant future. Should the dream become recurrent in nature, its motivational effects typically increase and its symbolic message acquires added significance.

Dream Condensation

Symbolism in dreams often reflects the creative brilliance of the subconscious through condensation, a common dream function in which large quantities of relevant information are reduced into a single dream symbol or event (TR-72). *Condensation* often represents a complex series of past events while predicting future developments. For example, a corporate executive's recurring dream of a vertical crack in the wall of the company's central administrative building resulted in his formation of an investigative team that examined the company's policies and practices. The results revealed several conditions that, if gone uncorrected, could have resulted in the financial collapse of the company. From the executive's perspective, his simple dream of a crack in the wall literally saved the company.

A closer look at the dream's dynamics, however, revealed a somewhat more complex picture that illustrates the extrasensory capacity of dream power. The dream's clairvoyant content revealed in symbolic form an existing condition of urgency, whereas its precognitive content predicted the company's future collapse should corrective action not be taken. Clearly, the executive's dream offers convincing evidence of functional dream symbolism as both an informative and motivational force.

Sequential Dream Symbolism

Somewhat similar to the executive's dream in which a crack in a building represented a corporation's instability, a husband's recurring dream of a house adrift at sea and spinning in a whirlpool was found to represent an unstable marriage which he described as "about to go down the drain." In his dream, the object (house) together with the action (spinning) conveyed a clear message in symbolic and condensed form: a marriage at risk. As the couple's conflicts were being jointly resolved through marriage counseling, his dreams became sequential in nature by accurately monitoring progress in the marital relationship. In his sequence of dreams, the spinning house became a floating house drifting aimlessly at sea. In his next dream, a tropical island at a distance came into view. In the final dream, the house came to rest upon the island, a clear signal that the marriage had survived (TR-72).

Dream Antithesis

Symbolism in dreams often includes *antithesis*, in which direct opposites are used to convey information of either present or future relevance (TR-72). For example, a dream of loss can signify gain, a dream of rejection can signify acceptance, and a dream of failure can signify success. Often predictive in nature, the antithetical dream typically presents a pertinent clue to its antithetical nature. For instance, an attorney dreamed of a guilty verdict for his client, a female who appeared as a male in the dream. The dream's gender reversal element provided a critical clue to the dream's true message: the guilty verdict antithetically predicted a not guilty verdict, a prediction that later proved accurate.

The purpose of dream antithesis is typically twofold: (1) it commands the attention of the dreamer, and (2), when needed, it motivates preventive or corrective action. That dual function of dream antithesis was illustrated by a college student whose dream of academic failure motivated her to improve her grade point average. She later graduated with honors. In a similar incident, the motivational effect of the antithetical dream was illustrated by a college student on academic probation who experienced a vivid dream in which he received at commencement a diploma with his name missing. The student's dream of a blank diploma generated a powerful motivational effect that resulted in significant academic improvement. He later graduated with honors (TR-72).

Therapeutic Symbolism

Among the common examples of the creative spontaneity of dream power are *therapeutic dreams* that convey relevant messages through creative symbolism (TR-126). While protecting sleep through symbols that disguise the message, therapeutic symbolism can seemingly convey relevant subconscious messages of both diagnostic and recovery relevance. That therapeutic function of symbolism was illustrated by the serial dream of an interior designer whose dream of an approaching tornado symbolized a turbulent personal relationship. As the tornado finally disappeared at a distance, the turbulence was replaced by peaceful serenity. While symbolically monitoring the relationship, the series of dreams effectively ventilated the stress related to it, a clear example of the therapeutic power of symbolism.

Therapeutic dream symbolism is often preparatory in nature as illustrated by a college student's recurring dream of an automobile stalled in heavy traffic that consistently preceded situations involving stress or threat. The predictive dream, by her report, provided nonthreatening information that increased feelings of security and confidence in her ability to cope with difficult situations.

The therapeutic dream message conveyed symbolically is seldom rejected by the dreamer. Determining the dream's therapeutic significance, however, is not always easy. A careful consideration of the dream's symbolic content not only facilitates understanding of the dream's message, but it can effectively unleash the dream's therapeutic powers related to it.

Free Association

Among the common methods used to facilitate interpretation of a given dream is *free association*, a technique in which a word or image related to the dream is used to stimulate the dreamer's spontaneous response, also in word or image form. The dreamer's response is then reflected upon and recorded in the personal dream journal. Perhaps not unexpectedly, the simple act of recording the response often increases understanding of the dream symbol, including the possibility of multiple meanings.

Free association is based largely on the concept that the personal characteristics of the dreamer along with situational factors typically interact to influence the dream experience

(TR-72). Consequently, analysis of the dream experience using free association can provide relevant information concerning the dreamer, including both personality and behavioral characteristics. For instance, dreams in which the dreamer is suddenly plunged into the dream action as opposed to dreams in which the action slowly evolves are often associated with a strong achievement drive and active pursuit of personal or career goals. Conversely, dreams in which the dreamer is a spectator are often associated with a more passive lifestyle as opposed to the dream experience of the more assertive individual who is typically involved in the dream as a participant actively influencing the action and outcomes.

Recurring Dream Symbols

Dreams with recurring elements, including objects, images, and themes of symbolic relevance, are particularly significant in that they are frequently associated with subconscious urgency to communicate messages of both present and future relevance (TR-72). The recurring dream, believed often to be associated with either an Achilles' heel or persistent threat, can continue for months or even years until finally the dream message is consciously perceived and acted upon. A law student experienced a frequently recurring dream of registering for a college course but forgetting to attend class until the scheduled final examination. He attributed the dream to stress associated with his studies;

however the dream persisted even after he had completed his law degree and entered a practice that unfortunately faltered. Seeking ways to improve his practice and sensing the possible relevance of his dreams, he began recording them in a daily dream journal. Finally, the significance of the recurring dream became evident: his disorganization along with his failure to give attention to details and to carry projects to their completion disrupted his effectiveness, whether as a student or practicing attorney. Acting upon the dream's message, he restructured his approach and developed a highly successful practice, whereupon the recurring dream ceased.

Summary: The Subconscious Knows

Through symbolism, the dream experience can become a seemingly unparalleled channel of power that conveys pertinent knowledge and reveals ways of effectively applying it. By accessing our personal past, addressing our present concerns, and probing our endless future, dream symbolism embodies four critical components: (1) It is *interactive* because it engages the inner sources of knowledge and power, from the highest levels of consciousness to the deepest levels of subconsciousness. (2) It is *extrasensory* because it reaches beyond the limits of conventional perception. (3) It is *interdimensional* because it engages other dimensions of knowledge and power. (4) It is *endless* because of its capacity to embrace the totality of personal existence—past, present, and future. Given these four critical components, dream symbolism when properly interpreted becomes effective in elevating dream power to its highest level.

Chapter 7
Dream Power Beyond the Ordinary

A moment's insight is sometimes worth a life's experience.
—OLIVER WENDELL HOLMES

The central focus of dream power in its finest form is upon the liberation and development of our highest growth potentials. Dream power beyond the ordinary recognizes the extraordinary capacity of dreams to dramatically push back the borders of awareness and conventional perception in ways that reveal totally new possibilities for achieving otherwise unattainable goals. Although that extraordinary capacity of dream power is often expressed spontaneously, it is receptive to innovative approaches that recognize its relevance to personal empowerment, including the successful achievement of highly challenging goals.

Dream power research conducted by PRIF consistently revealed the power of dreams to interact with extraordinary dimensions of knowledge and power (TR-150). Among those powers are dreams that extend awareness and unleash new knowledge beyond the commonly perceived limits of sensory perception. Included among those categories of extraordinary dream power are the following:

- Clairvoyant awareness of spatially distant realities
- Telepathic interactions with others
- Precognitive knowledge of future realities
- Retrocognitive awareness of past events and conditions
- Extradimensional interactions with outer realms as sources of knowledge and power
- Spiritual interactions, including interactions with spirit guides and growth specialists

Fortunately, you can purposefully experience each of these unusual phenomena through research-based dream power programs. Although these phenomena are known to occur during the dream experience as extraordinary manifestations of dream power, they are known to occur under other conditions, including normal wakefulness as well as hypnosis and various meditation states (Slate 1988).

The Flowing With Procedure

Among the programs designed to facilitate dream power beyond the ordinary is the Flowing With Procedure, a multifaceted approach that is largely a process rather than a procedure (TR-151). The procedure focuses on your capacity to work with your dreams as they work with you. It integrates autosuggestions and positive expectations into the dream experience to result in an effortless experience of *flowing with the dream*. The procedure is extraordinary: it activates dream power that dips far into the distant past and future alike. As you flow with the unfolding dream, you can experience the spontaneous power of dreams to reveal realities not commonly available to conscious awareness, while at the same time you can deliberately interact with the flowing process in ways that focus it upon your personal goals. That process, called Interactive Dream Intervention (IDI), thus becomes the dream's sentinel that adds both purpose and power to the unfolding dream experience.

The Flowing With Procedure can be particularly effective in promoting the extraordinary problem-solving functions of dreams. It can facilitate dreaming that increases awareness of existing conditions and possible consequences. For problem situations, the procedure can activate dream functions that reveal relevant causes and alternative solutions, each of which can be communicated either directly or symbolically.

The success of the Flowing With Procedure in the problem-solving dream is largely dependent on effective pre-sleep autosuggestion and the resultant *expectancy effect*. Among the most highly effective suggestions is the simple affirmation that workable solutions to specific problems will be forthcoming through dream power and remembered upon awakening. A positive expectation effect that promotes success is thus generated.

The following pre-sleep suggestions have shown unusual effectiveness in facilitating problem-solving dreams: *As I become drowsier and drowsier, I am becoming more and more aware of my hidden resources and higher mental powers. The solutions to the problems I am now encountering lie within myself. As I sleep, I will flow with my dreams as they lead me to those solutions. My dreams will be a source of insight, new knowledge, and power.*

As drowsiness deepens, highly specific affirmations of success are presented in strongly believable form and then concluded with the following suggestion: *As I flow with my dreams, I will remain open and responsive to their messages.*

Not unlike other dream experiences, the Flowing With dream often includes symbolism, condensation, antithesis, and other dream mechanisms that facilitate attentiveness and acceptance of the dream message while promoting quality sleep.

The Flowing With dream, like other dream experiences, often involves symbolism that is highly creative, as indicated in the dream of a college student nearing completion of her undergraduate degree in psychology. Faced with the difficult task of choosing between two equally appealing graduate schools, she decided to use the Flowing With Procedure in her effort to resolve the dilemma. Her description of the dream included what appeared to be elements of both dream power and out-of-body travel. By her report, the dream experience began with sensations of floating upward and away from her physical body at rest. Upon reaching what appeared to be a very distant location, she experienced an airborne view of the two universities, one to her left and the other to her right. As she viewed the scene from her aerial position, she turned the palms of her hands toward the university to her left, at which point it became increasingly dark. She then turned her palms toward the university to her right, whereupon it suddenly increased in brightness. Upon awakening, she knew clearly which university to attend. For her, the university enveloped in brightness represented both academic quality and future career success. She graduated with honors from the university and is today a successful psychologist in private practice. By her report, she continues her use of the Flowing With Procedure not only for herself but also with her clients when they face challenging decision-making situations (TR-151).

Dynamic Dream Power Program

Although each form of dream power holds empowering relevance, certain dream functions are profoundly extraordinary in their capacity to reach far beyond the conventional limits of personal experience. The Dynamic Dream Power Program (TR-152) is an advanced seven-step procedure developed by PRIF in an effort to expand the typical functions of dreams. Aside from that, the program is designed to facilitate direct intervention into the dream experience as it unfolds. When the program is properly implemented, the resultant dream experience can provide enlightenment concerning the past, present, and future through interactions with the subconscious as well as higher dimensions of power. Dream interactions with personal guides, guardian entities, and the departed are not uncommon during the Dynamic Dream Power Program.

A major feature of this program is the activation of dormant potentials related to pre-sleep reflection and personal goal statement. Here's the program:

Step 1: Pre-sleep Conditioning
Before falling asleep, take in a few deep breaths and while exhaling slowly, progressively relax your body from the

upper region downward. With your mind cleared of active thought, note the evolving presence of peace and serenity.

Step 2: Pre-sleep Reflection and Goal Statement

As drowsiness deepens, reflect on the extraordinary capacity of your dreams to exceed the boundaries of ordinary expectations. Reflect on your personal goals and your commitment to work with your dreams to achieve them.

Step 3: Hypnagogic Affirmation

Upon entering the brief transitional stage between wakefulness and sleep, sense the emergence of dream power and its capacity to influence the present and future alike. Again, state your intent to work with your dreams as they work with you.

Step 4: Dynamic Dream Interaction

As the dream experience emerges, engage it as a source of extraordinary power. While maintaining receptiveness to the unfolding dream experience, focus its power on shaping positive future realities, including those related to your growth and strivings.

Step 5: Extradimensional Enlightenment

Embrace the presence of spirit guides and empowering growth specialists as manifestations of higher realms of knowledge of power.

Step 6: Awakening Empowerment

Upon awakening, reflect on the dream experience and note its empowering effects, including the possible lingering presence of empowering guides and specialists.

Step 7: Dream Documentation

Record the experience in your dream journal.

———

This program typically requires considerable practice, but, once mastered, its empowering effects can be profound.

Extraordinary Phenomena: Research Validation

As earlier noted, dream power research conducted by PRIF consistently revealed the capacity of dreams to expand awareness beyond the conventional limits of sensory perception (TR-114). Traditionally, research into extrasensory phenomena has focused primarily on the nature and possible explanation of the so-called unexplained. With the emergence of validating evidence along with numerous theoretical explanations, more recent research has begun to explore the conditions conducive to these phenomena as potential sources of knowledge and power. Clairvoyance as the discernment of objects or conditions not present to sensory awareness appears to be among the major topics of contemporary dream research.

Among those research efforts was a study sponsored by PRIF at Athens State University designed to investigate the potential of dreams to initiate clairvoyance and convey clairvoyant information to conscious awareness (TR-117). The participants of the study were twenty volunteer students who used the Finger-Spread Technique to temporarily arrest the hypnagogic state just before falling asleep by spreading the fingers of either hand and, while maintaining that spread position, suggesting, *I will influence my dreams and benefit from them by the suggestions I now give myself.* Specific suggestions were then presented, whereupon the hand was slowly relaxed as the sleep state deepened.

The 20 subjects participating in the study consisted of 11 females with an age range of 19 to 26 years and 9 males with an age range of 20 to 25 years. All participants had previous experience in practicing the approach, typically in situations where a message, word, or number had been concealed in a dark brown envelope and placed either under the pillow or on a bedside table.

The experiment was conducted over a 10-day period, during which each participant of the study was presented a sealed envelope that contained a card with a number ranging from 1 through 9 written on it in black ink. Each participant was instructed to use the finger-spread arrest procedure as previously described to identify the concealed number. The specific autosuggestions presented during the arrest state were as follows: *As I drift into sleep, my clairvoyant powers will be activated. As I dream, I will see clearly the number printed on the card in the sealed envelope placed under my pillow (or on my bedside table).*

On the following day, the unopened envelope with the participant's identity of the enclosed card's number noted on the outside was returned to the project investigator. The envelope was then promptly opened and performance feedback was provided each participant.

On repeated trials over the 10-day period, the average performance of the group in accurately identifying the cards typically increased and was characteristically above that expected by chance alone. The results of the study showed a 55 percent accuracy rate over the 10-day period with 5 of the 20 participants successfully identifying the concealed card on all 10 trials. The remaining 15 participants achieved accuracy rates between 20 and 50 percent. In a replication of the study using Zener cards instead of numbered cards, the findings were similar. Whether using numbers or Zener cards, the groups using dream power consistently performed better than experimental control groups using no dream intervention technique.

The results of this study clearly illustrated the extraordinary capacity of dream power to reach beyond the conventionally imposed limits of human perception. The study further illustrates the capacity of hypnagogic intervention to activate that power.

Summary

Dream power beyond the ordinary illustrates the extraordinary capacity of dreams to probe the dormant inner sources of knowledge and power. Developing that extraordinary capacity, however, requires personal commitment and concentrated effort. The rewarding results can be well worth the effort. Included are the discovery of new knowledge, a surge of new growth power, and a deepening awareness of the meanings and mysteries of life.

Chapter 8
Advanced Dream Power

It makes all the difference whether one sees darkness through the light, or brightness through the shadows.

—DAVID LINDSAY

Dream power in its advanced form can be seen as both an art and a science. By exploring the subconscious interplay between art and science, it effectively accesses, organizes, and conveys knowledge of both scientific and artistic merit. Given the unique blend of art and science, dream power becomes a dynamic force that can transcend all constricting limits. It becomes the light of enlightenment and power that shines brightly through the darkness and shadows of the unknown.

Dream Power Advancement Plan

Advanced dream power focuses largely on research and ways of applying it to elevate dream power and enrich the quality of sleep. Numerous dream power studies, including those conducted by PRIF (TR-72), consistently show that what you experience during waking hours can generate a lingering residual effect that can influence sleep and the forthcoming dream experience. For instance, engaging in negative activities while you are awake, such as viewing violence on TV, can generate a *negative residual effect* that creeps into your dreams and diminishes the quality of your sleep. Conversely, engaging in positive activities while awake, such as expressing affection, tends to generate a positive residual effect that promotes restful sleep and constructive dreams (Slate 2009).

As a result of research designed to maximize the potentials of dream power, three sequential programs were developed by PRIF in which the positive residual effects of each program progressively increase (TR-118). The first two programs are implemented during the fully awake state, whereas the third program is initiated during the relaxed, drowsy state preceding sleep. The first program, an outdoor procedure called Star Gaze, is designed to generate an empowering interaction by viewing the starry night sky and centering attention on a personally selected star. The second program, called Moon Power, focuses on viewing the moon and interacting with it as a source of power. The third program, called Pinnacle Dream Power, incorporates the empowering effects of both Star Gaze and Moon Glow into an interactive pre-sleep program designed to advance dream power to its highest peak. There are many ways to elevate the power of dreams, but nothing seems more effective than the combination of these three interactive programs as follows:

Program 1: Star Gaze

This outdoor procedure called the Star Gaze Program is based on the simple premise that enlightenment is power. It embraces the concept that the greater your understanding of yourself and the universe, the more empowered you become. It is an energizing approach designed to focus attention on designated goals and empower you to achieve them. All that's required is the night sky with its display of stars and a willingness to interact with them. Should stars not be available for viewing, you can use an effective adaptation in which the starry sky is simply visualized. Visualized viewing, however, is typically more effective given previous practice in physically viewing the starry sky.

Apart from the residual effects of Star Gaze in promoting dream power, the program is applicable to an extensive range of personal goals. Similar in certain ways to the Flowing With approach, the program is both general and specific because it guides the dream experience toward designated goals while at the same time generating a state of self-confidence and success expectancy. The resultant *success destiny effect* typically lingers far beyond the dream experience to become a powerful force applicable to the achievement of other unrelated goals, including complex and long range.

The program as follows often results in profound awareness of the presence of a personal spirit guide.

Step 1: Star Scan

Before lying down to sleep, take time to view the night sky with its billions of stars. Scan the full sky and note your feelings of connectedness to it. View the variety in star characteristics, including the brightness of stars and the patterns they form. Remind yourself that among the billions of stars, no two are exactly alike.

Step 2: Star Selection

As you continue to view the night sky with its vast display of stars, reflect on your personal goals and select a star that seems relevant to them. As you center your attention on the selected star, note your increasing sense of connectedness to it. Think of that star as your link to the illimitable power of the universe. You may wish to give the star a name, any name that comes to mind. Note your sense of confidence in your capacity to achieve your personal goals.

Step 3: Star Glow Effect

As you continue to gaze at the selected star, slowly expand your peripheral vision to take in the full night sky from horizon to horizon. By then returning your focus to the selected star, you will note an expanded brightness enveloping it, a phenomenon called the *star glow effect*.

Step 4: Star Glow Interaction

While continuing to view the selected star with its expansive glow, turn the palms of your hands toward it as your connection to the limitless power of the universe. State your personal goals and affirm in your own words your power to achieve them.

Step 5: Conclusion

To conclude the program, view again the full night sky and reflect upon the empowering effects of interacting with it. Remind yourself that what you view before sleep can become a relevant part of your forthcoming dream experience.

———

Aside from generating a positive residual effect that promotes dream power, the Star Gaze Program is a highly flexible procedure that is receptive to an extensive range of personal empowerment goals, including academic and career success, effective stress management, resolving conflicts, and building self-confidence. Regular practice of the procedure tends to generate a dynamic interaction between the internal and external sources of personal empowerment. A political science student who often used the program noted that in the first session, Star Gaze put him in touch with the innermost part of his being and connected him to the highest powers of the universe. For him, the resultant sense of oneness and universal harmony increased with each subsequent session.

As PRIF research efforts continued over the years with participants of various age and background characteristics, the Star Gaze program was found to be among the most effective rejuvenation procedures known. Through regular practice, the program appears to activate both internal and external sources of rejuvenation. Dreams of being younger and more physically active became increasingly common among various age groups that practiced Star Gaze. Healthful changes in lifestyle are likewise frequently reported. A retired professor who regularly practiced the program reported that through Star Gaze, he discovered the secret of rejuvenation: simply select a star and interact with it.

Among the most remarkable functions of the Star Gaze Program is its capacity to resolve grief. A psychology graduate student whose mother had recently died in a traffic accident reported a powerful sense of her mother's presence upon viewing a selected star in step 2 of the program. She explained, "As I gazed at the bright star, I suddenly experienced a wondrous awareness of my mother's presence accompanied by the clear message 'It is well with my soul,' which was the title of her favorite hymn. It was a peak experience I will forever treasure" (TR-118).

The power of Star Gaze was also reported by a college student majoring in business administration. By her account of the experience, she noticed a bright point of light appearing briefly near the ceiling as she relaxed in her bed before falling asleep. As she viewed the point of light, she sensed at once the presence of her recently deceased father, whose favorite quote was that of Marcus Aurelius: "Look around at the courses of the stars, as if thou wert going along with them; and constantly consider the changes of elements into one another."

Program 2: Moon Power

The Moon Power Program is a nighttime exercise that focuses on the moon, preferably in its full phase, as a multifunctional channel of power (TR-118). In some ways similar to Star Gaze, it recognizes the empowering possibilities of reaching beyond our limited physical existence on earth and interacting with other dimensions of enlightenment and power. The program centers on the moon as the Earth's only natural satellite, with influences that appear to have made life possible on the planet. From that perspective, the moon's origin, a chunk of the earth hurled into orbit, set the stage for the evolvement of life on Earth. From another perspective, a higher force conceivably engaged the moon to initiate life on earth through its orbital effects. Given either perspective, the Moon Power program is designed to increase awareness and promote interaction with the highest sources of enlightenment and power. As in Star Gaze, awareness of a personal spirit guide often accompanies the program, particularly during step 5, Moon Power Embracement.

Here's the program:

Step 1: Preliminary Considerations

The Moon Power Program is a highly flexible goal-oriented procedure that requires a safe outdoor setting for viewing the clear night sky while either standing or comfortably seated. The procedure, which typically requires approximately fifteen minutes, can be practiced alone, with a partner, or as a group activity.

Step 2: Goal Statement

Prior to moon viewing, take a moment to reflect on your personal goals, whether short range or long term, and affirm your commitment to achieve them.

Step 3: Moon Viewing

Having specified your goals, clear your mind of active thought and focus your attention on the night sky with its extensive display of stars and the moon, preferably in its full phase. Should the moon not be available for viewing, the procedure is receptive to mental imagery in which the moon is visualized. This adaptation may require practice, but once the moon is clearly visualized, the procedure can be equally as effective as viewing the actual moon.

STEP 4: MOON CONNECTION
Having viewed the night sky, center your full attention on the moon. As you observe its features, including brightness, position, and other detailed characteristics, note your sense of connection to it.

STEP 5: MOON POWER EMBRACEMENT
While standing in the light of the bright moon, turn the palms of your hands toward the moon, and as moonlight falls upon them, note your increasing sense of connectedness to the moon as a powerful link to the universe.

STEP 6: HANDCLASP OF MOON POWER
As you continue to view the moon, slowly bring your hands together to form the *handclasp of moon power* as a manifestation of your connection to the moon and its power.

STEP 7: CONCLUSION
Conclude by relaxing your hands and affirming, *I am now fully empowered to achieve my highest goals.*

Beyond its positive residual transfer effects related to the dream experience, the Moon Power Program appears relevant to a seemingly unlimited range of personal empowerment goals. The program appears to be among the most powerful known for slowing aging and promoting rejuvenation. Both men and women, age seventy-five and above, who frequently practiced the program often reported a powerful infusion of rejuvenating energy during steps 5 and 6 with the turning of the palms of both hands toward the moon followed by the handclasp. The hands, they often concluded, served as the physical body's receptive antennae to the moon's rejuvenating power. In follow-up interviews with participants of this program, rejuvenation changes in physical appearance were clearly evident. By their own reports, the rejuvenating effects of the program progressively increased with regular use. Through repeated practice of the program, they became convinced that visualizing the moon was equally as effective as actually viewing the moon. The turning of the hands upward toward a visualized moon, they reported, generated tingling sensations of rejuvenation in the hands that then spread throughout the body. They were in full agreement that, having repeatedly practiced the program, they not only felt younger, but they also looked younger.

Aside from rejuvenation, the Moon Power program appears relevant to a host of other applications. Increased feelings of self-worth, awareness of a personal spirit guide, enlightenment concerning relevant past experiences, and relevant impressions related to the future are common. Detailed glimpses into the afterlife along with empowering interactions with the spirit realm often occur among individuals of various background and age characteristics. Students of various ages who practiced the program typically affirmed its effectiveness in accelerating learning and facilitating memory for materials learned. Whether practiced alone or with others prior to course examinations, the results typically included a marked increase in motivation and improved test performance. When practiced regularly by students, overall grade point averages typically improved.

As a self-empowerment procedure, the Moon Power Program has been highly effective in extinguishing fear, as illustrated by an athlete whose irrational fear of enclosed spaces severely limited the quality of his life. Following his first practice of the program, he appeared convinced that it exemplified moon power at its peak. As he viewed the full moon, by his account, a small cloud slowly appeared and partially concealed it. After lingering briefly, the cloud then gradually moved across the moon and disappeared into the distance, leaving the moon in full view and even brighter than before. As he viewed the moon, he reportedly felt at once a complete release of the fear of enclosed places that had plagued his life for years. The full moon with a small cloud crossing it was, in his view, all it took to permanently extinguish the fear and give totally new meaning to his life.

A clinical psychologist in private practice reported a vivid dream experience in which a glowing silvery shadow appeared on the ground next to her own as she viewed the moon. By her report, a few days later as she viewed the moon while practicing the Moon Power Program, a silvery shadow reappeared on the ground exactly as in her dream. She felt instantly connected to the glowing shadow as a spiritual presence. Over the years, the recurring manifestations of that presence have greatly enriched her life. As a result, dream therapy is today an essential component in her practice as a clinical psychologist (TR-118).

Program 3: Pinnacle Dream Power

The third program, called Pinnacle Dream Power, is a flexible program designed to incorporate the positive effects of the first two programs in ways that markedly elevate both the power of dreams and the quality of sleep. Initiated during the relaxed state preceding sleep, this goal-related program builds a powerful success expectancy effect through mental images and silent affirmations that incorporate the dynamics of both Star Gaze and Moon Power.

The results include an increased state of *empowered readiness* to the cognitive and affective elements of forthcoming dreams. Beyond that spontaneous effect, the program facilitates dreamer intervention into the dream experience as it unfolds. The dream experience can consequently become purposely directed to address specific mental, physical, and spiritual objectives or concerns. Optimal solutions to problems and accelerated mastery of new skills, including both artistic and scientific, have been known to occur as a result of managed dream intervention utilizing the Pinnacle Dream Power Program. Here's the program:

Step 1: Dream Preparation

Upon becoming relaxed before slipping into sleep, visualize the night sky with its multitude of stars and the moon in its full phase. Note your sense of oneness with the universe as the image of the night sky unfolds. Think of the moon and stars as orderly manifestations of power beyond that of any other source.

Step 2: Preliminary Dream Programming

As relaxation progresses and drowsiness ensues, take time to reflect upon your present life situation and personal goals. Allow relevant images of success to emerge as you quietly affirm, *Success is my destiny.*

STEP 3: MOON AND STAR POWER

As drowsiness deepens, visualize the moon along with its vast background of stars. Allow plenty of time for bright images of the moon and stars to unfold as you experience feelings of connectedness with them. With your attention centered on the evolving images, note the emerging sense of balance and attunement. Sense the vibrant infusion of power related to your present life situation and specific goals. At this stage, you may decide to focus your attention upon a particular star as a source of power related to a specific personal goal. You can increase the empowering relevance of the selected star by simply giving it a name—any name that comes to mind—as you experience an emerging sense of connectedness to it.

STEP 4: HYPNAGOGIC DREAM SHAPING

Upon approaching hypnagogic sleep, that brief state immediately prior to sleep, reflect again upon your goals as you silently affirm, *My dreams will provide me with the power I need to achieve these goals.*

STEP 5: PINNACLE DREAM INTERVENTION

As sleep deepens, visualize your goals and integrate them as essential components of the dream experience. Engage the dream experience as a multifunctional manifestation of enlightenment and power required to achieve your personal goals.

STEP 6: PINNACLE AWAKENING

Upon awakening, review your dream experiences and reflect on their relevance to your stated goals and life situation. Note particularly the past, present, and future relevance of your dreams. Sense the empowering effects of your dreams,

STEP 7: DOCUMENTATION

Document the dream by recording it in your dream journal

———

Pinnacle dreams are often accompanied by extended awareness of past, present, and future relevance. Examples include pinnacle dreams that retrieve relevant past-life experience related to growth blockages, irrational fears, and obsessive-compulsive behaviors. Interactions during pinnacle dreaming with spirit guides along with advanced growth specialists often characterize the pinnacle dream. Enlightenment related to distant realities along with increased awareness of pertinent past experiences, including those of past-life origin, are likewise common during pinnacle dreaming. Also characteristic of pinnacle dreaming are out-of-body experiences, including enlightening interactions with familiar spirit guides. Therapeutic interactions accompanied by the infusion of healing energy are likewise associated with pinnacle dreaming.

Growth barriers, including feelings of insecurity, irrational fears, and *free-floating anxiety* are often instantly extinguished through pinnacle dream intervention at step 5 of the program. A college student who practiced the program reported having experienced at that step not only the release of a long-term fear of failure, but also a clear image of herself being awarded a certificate of achievement for her humanitarian contributions. As it turned out, the student's dream proved to be precognitive in nature. During the university's commencement ceremony, she received special recognition for her humanitarian contributions (TR-118).

The Recurrent Pinnacle Dream

Both short-term and long-range goals are receptive to Pinnacle Dream Power. Pinnacle dreams are often recurrent and progressive in nature, a possible reflection of subconscious persistence in communicating insight related to challenging life situations. While maintaining its critical features, the recurrent dream can become progressively serialized through the introduction of changes that monitor progress while increasing awareness of future developments. In career settings, the pinnacle dream can provide insight that can promote progress and career satisfaction. In interpersonal relationships, the pinnacle dream can promote positive partner interactions that enhance stability in the relationship. Our controlled studies repeatedly showed that sharing the pinnacle dream experience with one's partner consistently enriched the relationship.

The Pinnacle Dream Cycle

Pinnacle dreams are often cyclic in nature (TR-118). As an inner-growth-oriented phenomenon, cyclic dream power is flexible because it can influence positive change, including progress toward achieving personal goals. It can increase motivation as well as the probability of success. That role of the pinnacle dream was dramatically illustrated by an investigative agent whose dream cycle began in the early stages of an investigation into the leakage of highly sensitive information of security relevance. In the early stages of the investigation, the agent's dream revealed the failure of certain security procedures and the absence of appropriate corrective measures. As the dream cycle progressed, it identified essential corrective and preventive measures. As a result, numerous critical changes were made in security procedures and related technology, all of which provided clear manifestations of pinnacle dream power in cyclic form.

Pinnacle dream power studies consistently show the interactive nature of the cyclic dream (TR-118). A positive psychological state can generate dreams that are optimistic in nature, whereas a negative psychological state can generate pessimistic dreams. Consequently, a cycle often develops with either positive or negative results. A depressed psychological state often results in depressive dreams that, unfortunately, increase depression in the post-sleep state. Similarly a highly stressful dream can predispose the dreamer to post-sleep anxiety, which in turn generates more stressful dreams. Fortunately, the negative cycle can be broken, and its negative influences can be offset or reversed through research-based procedures that promote positive dream and post-dream empowering effects. The Hypnagogic/Hypnopompic Intervention Program as follows is among the most effective programs known for achieving that important goal.

Hypnagogic/Hypnopompic Intervention Program

The Hypnagogic/Hypnopompic Intervention program is designed to maximize the power of dreams through intervention into both hypnagogic sleep, the brief transitional stage between wakefulness and sleep, and hypnopompic sleep, which occurs just before full wakefulness (TR-119). Although these two transitional stages are typically characterized by dreamlike images and sensations that appear to have little or no subconscious significance, they are important transitional stages that are receptive to purposeful intervention. Suggestions presented during the hypnagogic stage can significantly influence forthcoming dreams, whereas suggestions presented during the hypnopompic stage can influence the post-sleep state by promoting recall of the dream and reinforcing its effects. By working together, the hypnagogic and hypnopompic stages of sleep can maximize the empowering potential of the dream experience. This intervention program is designed to achieve that important goal. Here's the program:

Step 1: Goal Statement

Before slipping into sleep, reflect upon your personal goals and the relevance of dream power as a source of enlightenment and power related to them.

Step 2: Hypnagogic Arrest

As drowsiness deepens and hypnagogic readiness emerges, capture that brief transitional process by comfortably balancing your lower arm on the elbow in a comfortable, upward position. The beginning of the hypnagogic state is signaled when your arm begins to fall effortlessly to rest. By delaying the fall of the arm, the hypnagogic state is maintained, during which suggestions accompanied with visualization of success related to your stated goal are presented. Affirm your capacity to purposefully intervene into the dream experience and direct it toward your personal goals as previously stated.

Step 3: Dream Power Embracement

Embrace the dream process as it unfolds. Spontaneously flow with your dreams and interact with them in ways that focus them on your goals.

Step 4: Hypnopompic Embracement

Upon the emergence of hypnopompic sleep prior to full wakefulness, sense the empowering effects of your dreams, including those related to your goals and present life situation.

Step 5: Post-sleep Reflection and Affirmation

Reflect on your dreams and affirm their empowering relevance.

Step 6: Dream Journaling

Record the dream in your dream journal.

———

Always self-administered, the procedure's combination of hypnagogic and hypnopompic intervention has shown remarkable therapeutic potential for a wide range of therapeutic goals, among them the overcoming of depression. Clearly, dreams can influence our psychological state and personal adjustment just as our psychological state and personal adjustment can influence our dreams. Consequently, a cycle often develops. A depressed psychological state often results in a depressing dream, which in turn generates an increasingly depressed post-sleep state; likewise a highly stressful dream can predispose the dreamer to post-sleep anxiety, which in turn generates additional stressful dreams. Fortunately, the vicious cycle can be broken and the negative influences of such dreams offset or reversed by the combination of effective hypnagogic arrest (step 2) that focuses of positive, pleasurable dreams and hypnopompic embracement (step 4) that reinforces the effects of positive, empowering dreams.

The program has likewise shown remarkable effectiveness when used by couples, whether practiced jointly or independently, in overcoming barriers and increasing positive interactions.

The Dream Embracement Program

The problem-solving capacity of dreams is often spontaneously manifested, at times as a sudden "ah-ha!" dream experience that instantly provides insight, including workable solutions to complex problems. That problem-solving capacity of dream power is often illustrated by highly creative dreams that result in not only personal enrichment and success, but also global advancements, including technological and cultural.

Given the many reports of spontaneous problem-solving dreams, PRIF developed the Dream Embracement Program, which was designed to promote the multiple problem-solving functions of dreams (TR-127). The simple, easily administered procedure combines pre-sleep and post-sleep suggestions designed to access the subconscious solutions to specified problems and convey them to conscious awareness through the dream experience. The recommended pre-sleep suggestion presented as drowsiness ensues is simply a positive statement that productive and creative dreaming will occur. The follow-up hypnagogic suggestions state that solutions to specifically stated problems will be forthcoming through the dream experience and will be remembered upon awakening. Through autosuggestion, a positive expectancy effect is generated and allowed to be integrated into the dream state.

As a multifaceted approach, the Dream Embracement Program attempts to integrate autosuggestions and the resultant expectancy effect into the dream process in ways that generate an effortless embracement of the dream and focus it on desired solutions to problems. Should the free and spontaneous dream experience veer too far from the problem situation, dream embracement gently guides the dream back to the problem in ways that permit spontaneous dream continuity.

The success of the dream embracement process is largely dependent upon three essential factors: pre-sleep conditioning, relevant hypnagogic problem-solving suggestions, and the consequent expectancy effect. The following hypnagogic autosuggestions have proved highly effective in facilitating creative problem-solving dreams: *I am becoming more and more aware of my hidden resources and higher mental powers. The solutions to my problems lie within myself. As I sleep, I will embrace my dreams as they guide me to these solutions. My dreams will be a source of insight and new knowledge.* Highly specific suggestions relevant to problem situations are then presented in strongly positive, believable terms and followed with the concluding suggestion: *By embracing my dreams, I will discover new sources of power and how to use them to add enrichment and power to my life.*

Dream Embracement, not unlike other dream power programs, can include symbolism, condensation, antithesis, and other dream mechanisms that identify solutions and promote acceptance of them.

Summary

Through the programs presented in this chapter, you can experience the pinnacle of new power in ways that make the impossible possible. You expand awareness, dissolve growth barriers, and achieve an empowered state of growth readiness. You can reach beyond the most distant star of power and shine in the glow of moon power. You can make success your destiny.

Chapter 9
Creative Dream Power

Not in the clamor of the crowded street,
Not in the shouts and plaudits of the throng,
But in ourselves are triumph and defeat.
—HENRY WADSWORTH LONGFELLOW

The empowering potential of dreams is an inherent part of our existence as evolving beings. Dreams as the voice of the subconscious are influenced by a host of factors, including past experiences buried deeply in the subconscious along with current strivings, motives, conflicts, frustrations, and personal goals. Even subconscious awareness of relevant future events and distant realities can enter the dream experience to reveal relevant insight required for solving complex problems and effectively coping with difficult situations.

A major characteristic of dream power is creativity in which a variety of relevant factors are interwoven into the dream experience (TR-73). The goal of creative dream power is typically threefold: (1) to dissolve existing growth barriers, (2) to activate dormant growth potentials, and (3) to introduce totally new growth possibilities. That three-fold function of creative dreaming can occur in a direct, indirect, or mixed mode. In the direct mode, the dream is characteristically detailed, coherent, and realistic with little symbolism or other disguise. Conversely, the dream in the indirect mode is typically clothed in creative disguise that engages the dreamer's imagination. The dream in the mixed mode includes both direct and indirect elements in ways that clarify the dream and increase its empowering potential.

Among the major categories of creative dream power are dreams related to (1) creative insight, (2) inspiration, (3) therapeutic intervention, and (4) problem-solving, each of which can be a profound source of motivation and personal empowerment.

The Creative Insight Dream

The results of the creative insight dream range from increased awareness of potentials lying dormant in the subconscious to profound new insight related to personal identity and existence. Typically spontaneous, the creative insight dream is often recurrent or serial in nature. It can generate creative ideas, increase personal enlightenment, and motivate both personal and career development.

A college student preparing for a career in veterinary medicine reported a serial insight dream experience that began in his early adolescence (TR-73). In the first dream, he was standing on a ledge overlooking a vast wasteland below. There were barren trees everywhere, their limbs ominously jutting upward like spears. There was no movement or sound. He was repelled by the scene because there was no sign of life.

Throughout his adolescent years, the dream progressively changed as it monitored his career explorations. When he considered a career in agriculture, the forest became lush with plant life, but in subsequent dreams, the plants withered and died. As his interests turned to the military, the forest became a smoke-filled battle zone, and in subsequent dreams, it became a disquieting scene of injury and death. Finally, when he developed an interest in veterinary medicine, the dream became alive with vibrant scenes of both plants and animals. The satisfying dream, the last in the series, persisted as a stable recurring dream during his veterinarian studies to provide, in his opinion, a clear and creative confirmation of the wisdom of his career choice. He is today a practicing veterinarian who reports periodically experiencing the final dream in the series that, in his words, "adds to the rewards of being a veterinarian."

The Inspirational Dream

Through the creative dream experience, you can often discover not only your hidden potentials, but also the inspiration to develop them (TR-73). A journalist recalled an early lucid dream of writing with remarkable ease and spontaneous creativity. The dream became recurrent and continued throughout her childhood and adolescent years. Later, as a college student majoring in political science, she enrolled in an elective course in creative writing. Almost immediately, the creative potential as reflected in her past recurrent dream was unleashed. She chose to develop her writing potentials and is today a successful news journalist. She attributes both her success and career satisfaction in large part to the inspiration of her recurring lucid dream.

The Creative Therapeutic Dream

Creative dream power is often therapeutic because it provides the insight and power required to help dissolve growth barriers, including phobias and conflicts (TR-126). A college student reported a remarkable series of therapeutic dreams that eventually extinguished her fear of water. In the first dream, she viewed from a safe and comfortable distance a peaceful scene in which carefree bathers were playing happily on a beach. In the second dream, she was wading safely in the water. Finally, in the third dream, she was swimming without fear in the ocean. A vacation to the beach soon provided an opportunity for her to experience in reality her new freedom from fear of water. Although the series of dreams did not involve active intervention into the dream experience, the series did occur during a period of preparation for a vacation to the beach.

Unresolved conflicts, denied strivings, and repressed experience, including those reaching into early childhood, often seek resolution and relief through the therapeutic dream experience. Dreaming as emotional catharsis can effectively vent the pressures generated by repressed painful experiences, thereby empowering the dreamer to identify and work through the sources of the pain. Even a distressful dream experience can be a subconscious effort to liberate painful experiences stored in the subconscious.

The therapeutic nature of creative dream power reflects the remarkable capacity of the subconscious to promote personal development and enrich the quality of life. Understanding the therapeutic messages of our dreams and responding to the empowering efforts of the subconscious thus become critically important to self-realization and the actualization of our highest potentials. To be fully attuned to the subconscious and receptive to the creative power of our dreams may very well be one of the most important challenges we face in this lifetime.

The Problem-Solving Dream

Solutions to difficult problems often appear to reside in the subconscious, with dream power becoming the vehicle through which they are conveyed to consciousness (TR-139). The capacity of dreams to organize, assimilate, and convey information required for generating quality solutions is reflected by the fact that countless inventions and scientific breakthroughs have been attributed to the dream experience. Likewise, solutions to highly complex personal problems are often believed to originate in the subconscious, whereupon they are effectively conveyed to consciousness through dreams. That remarkable problem-solving efficiency of the subconscious may be due to its capacity to integrate past experiences and current insights into a creative dream function that merges conscious and subconscious resources in ways that result in a powerful creative interaction.

Dreams often motivate us to try on different roles and to experiment with various problem-solving procedures. When we are faced with indecisiveness, the problem-solving dream can function in ways that enable us to evaluate alternative approaches while providing valuable practice in successful problem-solving. Unlike the serial dream that often unfolds like a drama, problem-solving dreams are often like a series of one-act-plays, each independent and standing alone but laden with symbols requiring careful attention to details. The purpose of symbolism in such problem-solving dreams is typically threefold. First, symbolism allows the dreamer to experiment safely with even risky strategies in a manner that reduces anxiety or threat, thus permitting sleep to continue. Second, symbolism minimizes resistance to the dream message, thereby permitting the dreamer to play out the dream to its conclusion. Finally, symbolism invites conscious participation in unraveling and contributing to the problem-solving scheme.

Problem-solving dreams, frequently lucid in nature, appear devised to engage the conscious in a cooperative interaction designed to generate superior solutions. Although the subconscious often possesses information and insight essential to problem-solving, these resources are not always readily available to conscious awareness. Productive interaction between consciousness and subconsciousness through dream power can amplify and organize the resources existing at both levels of awareness to result in an advanced level of creative problem-solving that would not be possible by either alone.

Creative Dream Intervention

The creative functions of dream power are often initiated by the spontaneous intervention of daytime residue as well as pre-sleep programming techniques (TR-74). For instance, a fashion designer who visited an auditorium prior to a scheduled fashion event experienced a dream in which models appeared onstage wearing apparel of elegance unlike anything she had seen before. Her resultant fashion designs received widespread recognition as significant advancements in the fashion industry.

Aside from the spontaneous intervention of daytime residue, creative dream power can be deliberately activated through pre-sleep programming. For instance, a noted artist reports regular use of the pre-sleep suggestion that his artistic powers will become activated during sleep. The pre-sleep suggestion is followed by hypnagogic sleep intervention during which he visualizes a blank canvas accompanied by suggestions that, through dream power, designs would appear upon the canvas. His artistic creations resulting from this procedure have received international recognition.

Summary

Creative dream power can be seen as a flash of bright light appearing in the darkness. Through creative dream power, you can become empowered to see beyond the darkness and discover totally new dimensions of enlightenment and illimitable power. Fortunately, the creative flash of light as a channel of power is available to everyone.

Chapter 10
Multidimensional Dream Power

From wonder into wonder, existence opens.

—LAO-TZU

Multidimensional dream power is the capacity of dreams to engage and interact with both internal and external sources of personal empowerment (TR-115). The dream experience frequently complements our conscious efforts to gain relevant information or to find solutions to pressing problems. Almost everyone has experienced the "catch me if you can" dilemma, or seeking relevant information or solutions known clearly to exist somewhere but just out of the reach of conscious awareness. We diligently search for it, but somehow it evades our detection. With repeated effort, the information is often forthcoming, but when our conscious efforts are futile, the dream experience often spontaneously accesses and delivers the essential information, though often in challenging symbolic form.

Multidimensional dream power as an interactive phenomenon reflects the capacity of a specific dream function to promote the development of others. That observation, often called the *positive transfer effect*, implies that all mental faculties are related or at least possess certain common underlying factors. Research conducted under the auspices of PRIF identified certain conditions found to be highly conducive to multidimensional dream power (TR-115). These include:

- A positive self-concept that includes a sense of personal worth and well-being
- Recognition and acceptance of one's dream potentials
- Appreciation of the value of dream power
- Confidence in one's ability to influence the dream experience
- A success orientation
- Flexibility and a willingness to explore

Extrasensory Dream Power

Among the most common examples of multidimensional dream power are dreams of extrasensory relevance, including precognitive, retrocognitive, and clairvoyant dreams

(TR-116). Although numerous options exist to promote extrasensory enlightenment, the dream experience remains among the most highly effective. Whether spontaneous or deliberately induced, multifunctional dream power includes the capacity to activate the extrasensory potential existing in everyone. Always purposeful in nature, that capacity is known to utilize both direct and indirect mechanisms for conveying relevant extrasensory insight to conscious awareness.

Extrasensory dream power appears to exist within a framework that includes multiple inner functions. It can activate the precognitive, retrocognitive, and clairvoyant potential existing in everyone though often in dormant form. It can initiate telepathy, including its sending and receiving capacity. Aside from these, it can interact with other dimensions as sources of both enlightenment and power.

Precognitive Dream Power

The precognitive dream not only expands awareness of the future, but it can provide critical insight related to decision-making and planning that literally shape the future (TR-114). Even destiny is subservient to dream power in its purest form. Progress and future success in achieving personal goals are often linked to precognitive dream power as a source of knowledge not otherwise available to conscious awareness.

Precognitive dream power is typically multifunctional. It not only provides relevant information concerning the future, but it also facilitates preparation and possible intervention as well. Dreams predicting unbidden events or conditions often give clues related to intercepting or preventing the otherwise unexpected happening. For instance, a precognitive dream of an accident or injury may indicate the need for precaution, including alteration of plans. Should the predicted event or condition appear unalterable, the dream may indicate certain preparation or coping tactics. Many precognitive dreams, of course, concern enjoyable future happenings, thus providing pleasurable anticipation. Whatever the nature of the predicted event, the precognitive dream, like all dream power, is consistently purposeful and significant. When recognized and understood, it is a valuable source of information, enrichment, and growth.

Precognitive dream power is often goal directed. Its purposes, however, are not always immediately apparent due to the symbolism and other disguises frequently characterizing the precognitive dream process. Nevertheless, even the most highly disguised precognitive dream can become recognizable and meaningful, typically through introspection that identifies its relevance. A PRIF review of precognitive dream reports submitted by college students identified the following benefits of precognitive dreams (TR-114):

Preparation: Precognitive dreams often provide lead time essential to the preparation of future events.

Prevention: Precognitive dreams often suggest strategies for avoiding dangerous or high-risk situations and underside consequences as well as ways of preventing the actual occurrence of the predicted event.

Confirmation: The precognitive dream, once fulfilled, often confirms the wisdom or correctness of an important decision. Many major personal decisions are fraught with uncertainty and apprehension. Following such a decision, retro-awareness of a relevant precognitive dream can provide needed reassurance and support.

Motivation: The precognitive awareness of future success and the resultant success-expectancy effect can increase motivation, build self-confidence, and give the winning edge to future performance.

Enrichment: A broad perspective through precognitive dream power that spans the past, present, and future can become a source of deeper insight and understanding of the predicted event.

Solutions: Precognitive dreams are frequently problem-solving in nature, with the predicted event being the outcome of present strivings. Through precognitive dream power, more effective problem-solving techniques often emerge.

Almost everyone recalls a precognitive experience—a dream that came true, a premonition, or a persistent impression concerning a future event. The dynamics of the precognitive process, however, raise many questions concerning the nature of the future as well as the nature of precognitive dream power. Are certain future events fixed in time and thus predetermined? Does the subconscious have the capacity to perceive the future and convey precognitive awareness of it through dream power? Are certain future events, once consciously perceived, subject to personal intervention and altercation? Is the source of the precognitive experience internal, or does such awareness involve an external source, such as a personal spirit guide or growth specialist? These are among the questions that, once appropriately addressed, could help explain the precognitive dream and give insight into the dynamics of this interesting phenomenon.

The constellation of mental faculties existing in everyone does appear to include the capacity to experience awareness of the future independently of presently known predictive circumstances or realities. In explaining that phenomenon, the predestination view holds that certain events yet to occur already exist in unalterable form in the time dimension called the future. Another view assumes that certain future events yet to occur do indeed already exist, though in alterable form and subject to deliberate intervention as well as changes in present conditions. A middle-of-the-road explanation holds that while some future events are unalterably fixed in time, others exist in forms that are receptive to intervention and shifting conditions. Yet another view holds that the future is a dynamic, evolving phenomenon characterized by varying degrees of probability, ever dependent on the past and present.

Each of these views of the future assumes the existence of a time dimension energized by its very existence within a continuum of reality. Dream power holds that the relevant contents of that dynamic dimension could conceivably exist in transferable form through channels that include the dream experience. Although the dream experience can include the direct perception of the future in clear, undisguised form, it often consists of symbols along with bits and pieces of the future that are designed to protect consciousness from suddenly painful precognitions or to enhance acceptance of the information. From that perspective, the combination of symbols and precognitive bits and pieces can provide a full and complete subconscious picture of the future event.

Precognition through dream power can be seen as a normal extension of the human capacity for enlightenment and personal empowerment. The personal continuum of awareness—including past, present, and future—is dramatically extended through the precognitive dream experience.

The result is multidimensional dream power independent of commonly perceived limitations, including those related to time.

Retrocognitive Dream Power

While precognitive dream power engages the future, retrocognitive dream power engages the past (TR-174). It reflects the capacity of dreams to expand awareness of the past, including past personal experiences of present relevance. Not infrequently, the results include therapeutic insight sufficient to fully resolve the residual effects of negative past experiences, including those of past-life origin. Given enlightenment through the retrocognitive dream, you can often identify blockages and activate dormant growth resources required to help dissolve them. Examples include phobias, chronic depression, conflicts, persistent anxiety, and feelings of inferiority, to list but a few. Almost always, the empowering effects of retrocognitive dream power intervention are instant and complete. Given its record of success, retrocognitive dream power can be seen as among the most advanced psychotherapists.

Phobic conditions are particularly receptive to retrocognitive dream power that identifies their sources. The resultant insight often promotes alleviation of the phobia and its disempowering effects. Whether of current- or past-life origin, phobias function in the darkness of the unknown.

Once enlightenment shines upon it, the phobia often weakens and its disempowering effects are markedly reduced.

Deep-seated conflicts are likewise receptive to retrocognitive dream power. Once the source is uncovered through the dream experience, the unexplainable conflict becomes explainable. The dynamics of the conflict are often revealed through the dream experience in ways that help resolve the conflict. The results can be particularly effective in decision-making, including approach-avoidant situations that involve both positive and negative features. That dilemma was exemplified by a recently graduated business student faced with choosing between two job offers, each of which was characterized by both positive and negative features. In her dream, she viewed from above the two companies' headquarters situated side by side. Slowly, one headquarters began to fade away while the other began to glow progressively brighter. Upon awakening, she knew clearly which job offer to accept (TR-116).

Clairvoyant Dream Power

The clairvoyant dream connects awareness to spatially distant realities through the *dream-spatial fusion* process. The clairvoyant dream not only expands awareness of existing realities, but it also often intervenes in ways that promote positive change. A striking example of that dual capacity of dream power is a mechanical engineer's dream of a dangerous fault in a complicated manufacturing apparatus that resulted in a completely new design with a highly creative fail-safe feature. The new design was implemented, and the engineer received wide recognition for his creative contribution to the industry (TR-117).

Among the most important features of clairvoyant dream power is its capacity to monitor existing situations in ways that promote personal insight, often through the serial insight dream. That capacity of clairvoyant dream power was clearly evident in a series of three vivid dreams of a young engineer employed by a thriving industrial firm (Slate 1988). In the first dream of the series, he was driving his car alone on an arched bridge when suddenly the vehicle stalled and began to roll backward. He applied his brakes, but they did not hold. Finally, the car began to move slowly forward but failed to reach the top of the bridge. This first dream appeared to symbolically describe the engineer's feelings of insecurity and his struggle for advancement in the corporation.

In the second dream of the series, he was again driving alone on the bridge when as before the automobile suddenly stalled and began to move backward. He applied the brakes but as before they did not hold. He finally was able to start the car and move it a short distance forward, but again it stalled and began to roll slowly backward. He again applied the brakes, but they as before did not hold. Suddenly, he became aware that the arched bridge was incomplete. At its peak, there was a sharp drop-off into the river. He then realized that he was the only person on the bridge.

This second dream in the series seemed to further describe the young executive's feelings of insecurity and his struggle for advancement in the corporation. It introduced, however, a precognitive element: the incomplete bridge suggested a future career crisis and possible personal loss. While pursuing career success, his increasingly deprived social needs as symbolized by being alone on the bridge were threatening his personal well-being and future career success. His social interests were being replaced by "driving" career motives with resultant frustration in his personal and professional life. As a result of this second dream, he considered resigning from the corporation.

In the third and final dream of the series, he again was driving on the bridge but not alone. His vehicle did not stall as he drove freely forward in the traffic, a signal that the bridge was finally complete. He was relieved by the progress he was making. This final dream in the series seemed to indicate the need for certain corrective actions in his life, including the expansion of social interactions as symbolized by the other vehicles on the completed bridge.

Upon recognizing the clairvoyant messages of the three related dreams, the executive acted upon them. He began participating in a variety of career-related activities, including professional development programs that expanded his social interests and markedly increased his career success and satisfaction. The serial insight dream appeared to enrich his life by guiding him both personally and professionally beyond all previously self-imposed limits (Slate 1988).

Telepathic Dream Power

Dream telepathy as an interactive communication phenomenon is typically spontaneous. It can, however, be intentionally initiated through pre-sleep suggestion that includes content information as well as relevant imagery. It can include both cognitive and affective elements. Research sponsored by PRIF (TR-173) showed that dream messages of positive content can promote a positive mood state in both the sender and the receiver, whereas negative telepathic messages can generate a more negative mood state. These findings suggest a function of dream telepathy that reaches far beyond the mere transfer of information.

Similar to clairvoyance, dream power telepathy is often characterized by imagery and condensation that can convey far more complex and comprehensive messages than verbal messages alone. To facilitate communication, telepathic imagery can communicate ideas, feeling, or happenings in great detail. Condensation can, however, reduce the communication to a single image or symbol. In dream telepathy, a picture can indeed be worth a thousand words.

The sending and receiving of telepathic messages through dream power can include detailed information of both objective and subjective relevance. The message content can include emotions, sensations, and cognitions of both sensory and extrasensory nature.

Summary

Through the multidimensional dream, you can identify and activate a myriad of hidden growth potentials and accelerate their development. The multifunctional dream can promote awareness of the future and facilitate preparation for it; it can detect unseen conditions and identify their relevance; it can activate dormant potentials and stimulate their development; it can open new channels for more efficient interpersonal communication; it can enrich the overall quality of life. Given these myriad functions, multidimensional dream power becomes an illimitable force at promoting both personal and global advancement.

Multidimensional dream power reflects the transferable and interactive capacity of developmental dream power to create a personally empowered state in which the development of one mental faculty becomes readily transferable in ways that promote the awakening and development of other faculties.

Chapter 11
Global Dream Power

All the past is here present to be tried.

—HENRY DAVID THOREAU

Self-empowerment through dream power is a consistently positive developmental force that reaches far beyond the conventionally perceived limits of personal empowerment to include empowerment on a global scale. By focusing on personal needs and the struggle for significance and meaning, dream power can become a continuous growth process that awakens dormant potentials and increases the capacity to develop them. The multiple programs presented in this book are designed to promote that two-fold process.

The Comprehensive Dream Power Plan (TR-174) consists of the following three programs that are designed to interact in ways that (1) generate a state of personal attunement and balance, (2) maximize the power of dreams, and (3) address global concerns. Here are the programs:

Program 1: Attunement Activation Program

The Attunement Activation Program is a self-administered step-by-step procedure designed to generate attunement and balance among multiple functions, both mental and physical. Here is the procedure, which is administered while resting comfortably in a quiet, safe setting free of distractions or interruptions:

Step 1: Clearing

Clear your mind by centering your thoughts on your breathing. Feel the air soaking into your lungs, your chest expanding and contracting as you breathe deeply and rhythmically. Take plenty of time to develop a comfortable, rhythmic breathing pattern.

Step 2: Imagery Flow

Become so absorbed in your breathing that you are aware of nothing else; then allow peaceful imagery to flow in and out of your mind. Note the color, movement, and detail of your imagery, but do not attempt to arrest it. At this stage, simply allow the images to come and go spontaneously.

Step 3: Imagery Selection

From among the images flowing through your mind, select one that seems right for you at the moment and focus your full attention on it. Become so absorbed with the image that you seem to lose yourself in the process. Stay with the imagery until you have fully absorbed its energies.

Step 4: Attunement

Let the imagery dissolve away until nothing remains. Your mind is now emptied of all voluntary or spontaneous imagery or thought. The process of your being is now neutral, synchronized, and balanced inwardly and outwardly.

Step 5: Conclusion

Conclude the procedure by affirming, *I am now fully attuned, both inwardly and outwardly. My total being is infused with powerful growth energy. I am now empowered to actualize my highest potentials and achieve my highest goals.*

Program 2: Inner Dialogue— Activating Dream Power

Dream power is consistently receptive to positive inner dialogue that recognizes self-worth and the potential for success. Whether presented before sleep, upon awakening, or in daytime, positive inner dialogue can activate dream power and effectively focus it on designated goals. When presented in either silent or vocal form, positive inner dialogue before sleep can initiate dream power relevant to existing conditions and future goals. When presented upon awakening, it can reinforce the power of dreams. When presented during waking hours, it can further elevate dream power and increase its empowering effects.

Through empowering inner dialogue that recognizes personal worth and the potential for continuous growth and success, dream power becomes an increasingly dynamic force of both present and future relevance (Slate 1991). Following are examples of inner dialogue with potential to lift dream power to its highest level:

- *I am a person of worth.*
- *I believe in myself and my power to succeed.*
- *I am capable and secure within myself.*
- *I have the power to achieve any goal.*
- *I can overcome any barrier and meet any challenge.*
- *Nothing can deter me from succeeding.*
- *I am destined for success.*

Both of the aforementioned programs recognize dream power as a dynamic growth and enlightenment process. They focus on our personal needs and the struggle for significance and meaning. Like other programs presented in this book, they are designed to awaken dormant capacities and activate the self-empowerment potential existing in everyone.

Program 3: Global Dream Power

In possibly its most advanced form, dream power can transcend the self and address global concerns. Because self-empowerment through dream power is both growth and action oriented, it can deal with such issues as world hunger, poverty, injustice, abuse of animal and human rights, discrimination, pollution, and reckless exploitation of our natural resources

Simply reflecting on global concerns during the drowsy state preceding sleep is often sufficient to activate dream power of global relevance.

Among the global issues considered relevant to dream power are the following:

- A growth-fostering world that moves us toward a more worthwhile life for all
- Global harmony that flows from a new understanding of the rights, dignity, and worth of each human being
- A new wave of compassion and trust
- An end to poverty, hunger, discrimination, and inequality.
- A solution to global strife and unrest
- A new caring and nurturing of animals

- An end to global pollution and reckless depletion of natural resources
- A genuine concern for others, including populations that are to follow us

Each of these goals is receptive to dream power of both individual and group origin. When members of a group collectively use dream power to address specific global concerns, a powerful group effect can be generated that magnifies the sum of individual efforts.

Personal Choice

Personal choice is the cornerstone of dream power. Through your decisions, you can influence the present and help shape the future. Future realities are, in fact, often the direct products of personal choices. The most effective self-empowerment procedures not only expand your potentials, but they also increase your options for choosing as well. Through recognizing those options and responsibly choosing among them, you can assume command of your life at the moment and influence the future consequences of your existence.

Summary

The state of being self-empowered through dream power is a never-ending process of growth and self-discovery. As a self-empowering force, dream power challenges each of us to press forward with purpose and determination. As an endless process, it can give new meaning and power to our existence in the present and future alike. Through a deeper understanding of the self through dream power and by being who and what we are in the moment, we can experience an empowered state that authenticates our existence and validates our being in the world.

Chapter 12
The Five-Day
Dream Power Plan

Self-empowerment through the dream experience is available to everyone. The techniques of dream power presented in this book can be applied to enrich life, promote personal success, and even bring positive change into the world. Becoming self-empowered, however, requires choosing which skills to acquire, how to use them, and for what purposes. A strong sense of personal responsibility and a willingness to explore along with a firm belief in oneself thus become among the major factors required for maximizing the power of dreams.

In previous chapters of this book, many aspects of dream power are examined, and step-by-step procedures are developed to activate the empowering potentials of dreams and focus them on desired goals. Several barriers to dream power, some deeply rooted in our culture, were exposed, and ways of overcoming them were put forward. A wealth of research shows that for too long we have functioned with low power, and too often we have failed to take decisive steps to promote our personal growth and self-empowerment. The Five-Day Dream Power Plan (TR-191) consists of a progressive five-day series of programs, each designed to empower you to work more effectively with your dreams as they work with you. It is a flexible plan that includes advancements related to personal growth, including skills related to successful goal preparation before sleep, intervention as needed during sleep, and reflection after sleep. The plan is designed to access inner as well as outer sources of both knowledge and power. Equally as important, it is designed to facilitate memory of the dream and enlightenment concerning its relevance, including past, present, or future.

The Five-Day Dream Power Plan addresses multiple components of dream power and organizes them into a structure that is both multifaceted and multifunctional. Designed to promote development of the wide-ranging potentials of dreams, it focuses on dissolving barriers and activating latent dream power resources. By promoting an empowered state of inner balance and readiness to dream power, the plan evokes a spiraling process that generates a positive state of receptiveness to dream power both during and after sleep. Once activated through the plan, dream power can become increasingly effective in accelerating personal growth and promoting success in achieving an extensive range of personal goals.

The Five-Day Dream Power Plan recognizes the complex dynamics underlying dream power along with the wide range of individual differences in preferences and potentials. It is a flexible plan designed specifically to maximize the diverse empowering functions of the dream experience. It consists of both preparatory and implementation elements as well as daytime wakeful components that enter sleep in ways that influence dream power. It includes pre-sleep components that likewise influence quality sleep and dreams. It also includes post-sleep components that review the dream experience and reflect upon its relevance. Finally, the plan as follows focuses on the interactive capacity of dreams to promote quality of life and a generalized state of self-empowerment.

Each program in the plan is flexible and readily adaptable to your personal goals and needs.

Day 1: Stairway to Power

Day 1 of the Five-Day Dream Power Plan introduces a meditation exercise that combines visualization and self-affirmation in ways that promote dream power as a positive interactive component of full self-empowerment. The Stairway to Power Program recognizes the interactive nature of dreams and the relevance of dream power to each step in the stairway. It identifies certain basic characteristics—peace, harmony, forgiveness, and faith—that are conducive to dream power—while also emphasizing the importance of choice and change. Awareness and knowledge are the steps that finally lead to self-empowerment as a dynamic developmental process. Following are the program's nine steps, each with relevant affirmations:

Step 1: Inner Peace

Inner peace is like a river flowing throughout my total being. It is deep, abiding, calm, and secure. It gives quality and wholeness to my existence. Given inner peace, I can cope with any storm or turbulence that enters my life. Misfortune, disappointment, hardship, and uncertainty all yield to the quieting comfort of inner peace.

Step 2: Harmony

Harmony in my life empowers me to be spontaneous and free. My thoughts, feelings, expectations, goals, and actions are integrated and balanced into a harmonious system of interactive functioning. They all work together to promote my full growth and liberate the dormant potential within my total being. Through a balanced, harmonious state of mind, body, and spirit, I am empowered.

Step 3: Awareness

Through increased awareness of my total being, my life is enriched with new insight of past, present, and future relevance. The purpose and meaning of my life is clarified as I become face to face with the totality of my being in the here and now.

Step 4: Faith

Faith is the elevating force in my life. It lifts me to new heights of power. It is my belief in my own being and the quintessence of my existence—past, present, and future. It sustains me in adversity and motivates me to forever press forward.

Step 5: Change

Change is the stream of progress. It carries me always forward to reveal something vital to my existence. To become more energized, enlightened, and compassionate—all are changes I value. Positive change carries me always forward to reveal something new about my existence.

Step 6: Knowledge

Knowledge enriches my life with new meaning and power. It empowers me to accelerate my own growth and assume greater command of my own destiny. Through knowledge, I become empowered to set personal goals and effectively achieve them.

Step 7: Choice

I experience choice each moment of my life. I choose to think or not to think. I chose to act or not to act. I choose to feel or not to feel. Because I choose, I am responsible for my thoughts, feelings, and actions. They belong to me and I am responsible for them. I am what I choose to be. The state of my being in the moment is the result of my choices.

Step 8: Love

Love is essential to my life. It is the energizing center of my being. In my capacity to love, I discover myself and add meaning to my existence. Love is the most powerful expression of my being.

Step 9: Self-Empowerment

Through inner peace, harmony, awareness, faith, change, knowledge, choice, and love, step by step I become fully empowered to develop my highest potentials and achieve my highest goals.

Day 2: Success Conditioning Program

The Success Conditioning Program, day 2 of the five-day plan, is a pre-sleep exercise designed to strengthen an evolving self-empowering orientation that is conducive to dream power while building a powerful success expectation effect. The five-step program is initiated by supportive, positive suggestions presented in the relaxed, receptive state preceding sleep. As a goal-oriented program, the program often results in dreams that build feelings of self-confidence and increase the probability of success. The procedure has shown unusual effectiveness in breaking unwanted habits, solving personal problems, mastering special skills, and overcoming barriers to success.

After at least one goal is formulated, the Success Conditioning Program is implemented as follows:

1. Dispel negativism and saturate your mind with positive thoughts. Visualize your body being enveloped by a radiant light of powerful energy permeating your total being with pure energy.

2. Specify your goal and picture yourself successfully attaining it. Clearly visualize yourself in the successful goal attainment situation. Note your sense of success, confidence, and security.

3. Immerse yourself as completely as possible with impressions, sensations, and clear images of success in the future goal-attainment situation. As you interact with the situation, blend yourself completely—mind, body, and total being—with a powerful awareness of success.

4. Imagine a channel of light connecting your energy system to the success situation. Keep the channel open for the flow of positive energy.

5. Claim the goal as already yours. Maintain the image of yourself in the successful goal attainment situation as you work with confidence toward your goal.

Aside from its use as pre-sleep or post-sleep exercise, this program can be easily adapted for practice as a daytime meditation exercise.

Day 3: Hypnagogic/Hypnopompic Power Program

Day 3 of the Five-Day Dream Power Plan initiates a self-empowerment program designed to help you access new sources of dream power and to intensify inner processes for the discovery of new insight and understanding. An empowering dialogue can be effectively initiated during the hypnagogic transition state between wakefulness and sleep as well as during the hypnopompic transition state between sleep and wakefulness. With each individual in a state of empowered readiness during the transitional states of sleep, the inner sources of insight and knowledge await self-empowering efforts.

Suggestions presented during hypnagogic sleep typically require a brief arrest of this earliest state of sleep. The Finger-Spread Technique of simply spreading the fingers of either hand and briefly holding the spread position is usually sufficient to briefly arrest hypnagogic sleep, during which empowering suggestions similar to the following are presented: *As I drift into peaceful sleep, I am renewed and infused with harmonious, balanced energy. During sleep, my inner growth potentials will generate new possibilities for insight and understanding. My dreams will become a source of new growth energy and empowering knowledge. I will awaken refreshed, energized, and empowered.*

The following are examples of empowering hypnopompic affirmations: *My inner powers are now at my command. I am empowered to meet today's challenges and to solve today's problems. I have full confidence in myself and my abilities. Today I will experience self-discovery and self-appreciation. I value the things I discover about myself. I value being myself.*

These hypnopompic affirmations can be effectively reinforced when repeated as a fully awake exercise that activates and further develops them. Through the practice of this exercise, positive inner dialogue becomes increasingly effective at calling forth relevant coping resources.

The Hypnagogic/Hypnopompic Empowerment Program is among the simplest yet most empowering program known for purposefully activating dream power and reinforcing its effects.

Day 4: Empowerment Stabilization Program

Day 4 of the Five-Day Dream Power Plan is based on the premise that your potential for personal empowerment and success can be enlarged and your evolving empowerment functions reinforced through your development of new dream power skills. The Empowerment Stabilization Program, also known as the 3-A Plan, is designed to promote a constant state of empowerment readiness and success expectancy, both of which are critical to the development and stabilization of self-empowerment skills, including those related to dream power. Essentially meditative in nature, the program requires a comfortable, quiet setting free of distractions. It can be applied prior to sleep, upon awakening, or during the day.

Empowerment Attitude: A positive attitude of empowerment determination is firmly established through positive affirmations such as these: *I can settle for nothing less than full empowerment. I am assuming a position of personal empowerment in my daily activities. I am empowered to meet any of life's demands. Complete success is my destiny.*

Empowerment Authorization: Inner power resources are recognized, authorized, and activated through such dialogue as this: *I give myself permission to use my inner power resources. They are working with me as I work with them. They are enabling me to function effectively and confidently as I interact continuously with them.* Inner power sources are specifically accessed and authorized to achieve particular objectives as the need arises.

Empowerment Attentiveness: Through inner dialogue, a constant state of empowerment attentiveness is maintained. Awareness is periodically focused on the empowerment process itself as positive affirmations are formulated. The simple reminder, *I am empowered,* is usually sufficient to stabilize and maintain the empowering infusion process at a steady pace.

Through the application of this three-component program, a stabilizing empowerment effect can be established with results that maximize the effectiveness of your self-empowerment efforts. Given Empowerment Attitude, a mental state conducive to empowerment is firmly established. Given Empowerment Authorization, empowerment becomes an authentic reality. Given Empowerment Attentiveness, empowerment continues as a vital growth and development process.

Day 5: Orb of Energy Program

The program for day 5 of the five-day plan is essentially a meditative approach that begins by focusing on the solar plexus, that central abdominal region that radiates energy to encompass the full body and beyond. It is designed to generate a dynamic, interactive sphere of energy enveloping the full body (TR-193). The program called Orb of Energy can be administered as either a pre-sleep or a daytime program. The results are an attuned, energized state that is highly receptive to dream power. The four-step program as follows requires approximately thirty minutes while resting comfortably in a secure setting free of distractions.

Step 1: Relaxation

While resting comfortably in a reclining or semireclining position, take in a few deep breaths, and while exhaling slowly, notice the relaxation first in your solar plexus and then spreading throughout your full body. Take plenty of time to develop a slow, rhythmic breathing pattern as you become more and more deeply relaxed, from your forehead to the tips of your toes. Become fully relaxed.

Step 2: Solar Plexus Concentration

Focus your attention on your solar plexus as the energizing core of your being. Visualize bright energy as an orb of light situated in your solar plexus and from there radiating bright energy throughout your full body.

Step 3: Orb of Energy

Sense the infusion of bright energy radiating beyond your body and enveloping it with a glowing sphere of energy. Note your interaction with the sphere of energy as an external manifestation of your inner center of energy. Note the dynamic features and functions of the sphere and your capacity to interact with it.

Step 4: Orb Interaction

Given increased awareness of the orb and its empowering relevance, take time to interact with it as an integral component of your being. Embrace the orb as a manifestation of your higher self. Sense the power of the orb to connect you to the higher sources of knowledge and power existing both within your own being and beyond, including higher realms of power. You may at this point sense the presence of spirit guides or guardians and their receptiveness to your interactions.

———

The Orb of Energy Program is especially receptive to the interactive presence of spirit guides, guardians, and growth specialists. Solutions to personal problems, dissolution of growth barriers, and discovery of totally new growth resources are not uncommon among the results of this program whether used either as a pre-sleep or daytime exercise. Practice of using the program and reflecting upon it can dramatically increase its effectiveness.

Summary

Dream power, rather than something you possess, is an essential part of your existence. It is a manifestation of the endless nature of your being and your capacity to become far more than you are. Through the Five-Day Dream Power Plan, you can acquire the skills required to reach beyond all self-imposed limitations and engage totally new sources of enlightenment and growth. You can, in a word, become *empowered*!

Conclusion

The power of dreams is immeasurable and unending. Even the seemingly negative or disempowering dream experience can become a source of power that resolves conflict, motivates achievement, and promotes success in achieving the otherwise unachievable. The power of dreams can reach into your endless past and endless future alike to engage new sources of power relevant to the present. It can activate the power required for the realization of your highest potentials.

Fortunately, dream power is available to everyone. Aside from its frequent spontaneous manifestations, it can be developed to its peak through the detailed programs and plans presented throughout this book. Even a highly specific gesture, such as a simple pre-sleep cue, can activate dream power of profound relevance. Deliberately designed step-by-step programs can promote the actualization of dream power and effectively focus it on designated goals. Even global advancement is receptive to dream power through such intervention programs as the Comprehensive Dream Power Plan.

Whether spontaneous or deliberately activated through specially designed dream power programs and techniques, dream power is a positive, empowering force that is both infinite and transcending. A greater understanding of dream power as an inner developmental force along with the application of specially designed programs that interact with it are together essential to our personal empowerment and the advancement of humanity.

Glossary of Dream Symbols

Because the relevance of a specific symbol can depend on a host of influencing factors, any listing of dream symbols and their potential meanings is risky at best. Nevertheless, the meanings of many symbols do appear reasonably stable. For instance, upward motion in dreams typically signifies progress, whereas downward motion typically indicates failure or the need for corrective action. Viewing familiar settings from overhead, including those associated with the distant past, typically suggests the need for objectivity in resolving past concerns and coping with present demands.

Dreams are made more complex when they include an amalgamation of symbols including objects, actions, and settings, each of which possesses symbolic significance. For instance, a dream of a distant sinking ship includes action (sinking), object (ship), and setting (distant) with the action possibly symbolizing loss, the object symbolizing opportunity, and distance representing time. A sinking ship at a great distance would therefore suggest lost opportunity some-where in the distant future, whereas a sinking ship close at hand would suggest the predicted event is imminent.

This listing of dream symbols and their suggested meanings is based largely on case studies and research-based findings related to the underlying dynamics of dream power. As noted in the listing, a given symbol can have multiple meanings and functions. Among the major influencing factors are past experiences and their residual effects, unresolved conflicts, personal relationships, goal-related strivings, and existing adjustment demands. The listing is offered not to constrict the meanings of dream symbols but to suggest possibilities and to illustrate the value of symbolism in dreams as a source of personal insight and power.

Determining the relevance of a particular dream symbol is often a difficult needle to thread. Although accurate interpretation of the symbol can be spontaneous, it often requires a consideration of the dream's objective or manifest content as well as its latent content and subjective implications. Further complicating interpretation is the dream's use of *antithesis*, in which a particular symbol represents its direct opposite. For instance, *confined* can represent *liberated*, whereas *airborne* can represent *grounded*. As a dream mechanism, antithesis typically promotes both acceptance and recall of the dream experience. Given awareness of the dynamics of symbolism and its relevance to personal and situational factors, you, the dreamer, can become the best interpreter of your dreams. Developing that potential, however, requires receptiveness to dream power as well as persistence.

Among other factors affecting the relevance of dream symbols are a variety of situational factors, including the day of the week in which the dream occurs. Dreams occurring early in the week are typically achievement oriented and tend to relate to long-range goals and career concerns. On the other hand, dreams occurring later in the week or on weekends are more likely to be pleasure oriented and related to immediate goals and personal relationships. Colorful, adventurous dreams, likewise, tend to occur toward the week's end.

Dream power is a manifestation of the life force that characterizes our existence as forever evolving. It embraces the endlessness of our past and future alike. As a developmental force, it reaches from the highest levels of consciousness to the deepest levels of subconsciousness. Given a greater understanding of our dreams, we can experience a greater understanding of our existence—past, present, and future.

Through the list of dream symbols that follows and the examples of meanings associated with them, you can expand your understanding of your dreams as sources of enlightenment and power (TR-180).

Dream Symbol and Suggested Meanings

A

abandoned: insecurity, self-rejection, lack of self-confidence

abyss: emptiness, challenge, the unknown

accident: loss of innocence, the need for caution, broken relationship

acrobat: uninhibited, free, playful

anger: frustration, emotional ventilation, self-rejection, loss of control

animal: affection, friendliness, peace, need to nurture

armor: protection, security, uncertainty

auditorium: the social self, social interest, social activity

avalanche: urgency, the need for immediate intervention

B

badge: courage, recognition, honor, striving for success

ball: completeness, exploration, pleasure

banner: need for recognition, striving for integrity

barn: constricted social interest, greed, inferiority feelings

bird: impulsiveness, spontaneity, self-actualization needs

blindness: deprivation, challenge, uncertainty

boat: journey, work in progress, opportunity, escape

body, physical: health concerns, perceived helplessness

book: knowledge, enlightenment, self-discovery

box: self-contained, boxed-in, restricted, inadequate

bridge: transition, escape, link, new opportunities
butterfly: gentleness, vulnerability, a new beginning

C
candle: reason, intelligence, honesty
cathedral: aspiration, hope, power
cavern: emptiness, the unknown, hidden
ceremony: transition, reward, change
chase: escape, vulnerability, impulsivity, aggression
child: innocence, honesty, escape
city: interpersonal relations, opportunity, change
classroom: opportunity, control, constrictions
climbing: motivation, escape, progress, exploration
cross: sacrifice, conflict, hope
color: creative potential, motivation, achievement needs
construction: new interests, new opportunities, situational change
conversation: desire for intimacy, search for solutions
crash, auto: uncertain conditions related to social conditions and career situations
crying: search for fulfillment, emotional relief

D
dancing: escape, carefree, uninhibited
death: change, loss, surrender
desert: the innermost self, search for meaning, escape

driving: progress, self-discovery, achievement, independence

divorce: conflict, self-rejection, ending, disconnect

document: strong resolve, recognition needs

door: new opportunity, escape, discovery

drowning: desperation, loss of control, self-defeat

E

earthquake: personal loss, vulnerability, impulsivity

eating: gratification, pleasure, sexual desire

enemy: alienation, fear, rejection

entrance: new beginning, discovery

exercise: self-improvement, strengthening coping abilities

explosion: lost opportunity, sudden termination, failure of a plan, emotional catharsis

F

failure: abandonment, survival, a new beginning

falling: illness, stressful situations, liberation, survival, insecurity, loss of control

family member: responsibility, obligation, conscience

fence: barrier, separation, isolation

fighting: struggle, hostility, negative impulses

fire: passion, aggression, failure, lost opportunity

firearm: hostility, fear, greed, aggression, self-destructive tendency

fish: escape, evasive tendency

flood: caught off guard, overwhelmed, adjustment difficulty, insecurity

flower: serenity, affection, pleasure, gala affair, abundance

flying: search for meaning, astral travel, longing for escape

football: competitive struggle, aggression, strong achievement drive, assertiveness, independence, endurance

fog: uncertainty, procrastination, shortsightedness, danger

fortress: defensiveness, protection, security needs

friend: trust, stability, contentment

fruit: desire for friends and meaningful relationships

G

gem: discovery, insight, wisdom, prize

gift: pleasure, discovery, good fortune

H

hiding: fear, guilt, withdrawal

holiday: freedom, pleasure, relief

horse: need for power and control

house: family interests, social concerns

humor: positive outlook, optimism, escape

I

ice: inflexibility, difficulty coping with stress, arrested development

infant: renewal, innocence, a new beginning

injury: psychological vulnerability, anxiety, personal insecurity, failure

island: safety, security, isolation, social withdrawal

invitation: adventure, recognition, approval

J

jewelry: caring, commitment, resolution, security, devotion

journey: change, search, uncertainty

jungle: complexity, entanglement, risk

K

kissing: love, desire, commitment

knife: anger, protection, aggression

L

ladder: strong achievement drive, ambition, determination

lake: escape, unknown, search

lantern: skepticism, self-orientation, limited insight, constricted interests

laughter: self-acceptance, sense of humor, adaptability

leash: control, inhibition, reserve

letter: inner attunement, enlightenment, search for meaning

light: knowledge, signal, hope, important breakthrough, protection

lightning: external intervention, unpredictable consequences, impulsivity, disorganization

M

metal: inflexibility, fixed perceptions

mirror: introspection, exhibitionism, constricted perceptions, isolation

mob: opposition, upheaval, uncertainty, loss of control

money: material interests, financial concerns, strivings for power and recognition

monster: fear, insecurity, vulnerability to threat

moon: romance, mystery, strength, security

motion: change, progress, search

mountain: barrier to success, challenge, opposition

music: harmony, balance, pleasure, inner peace

musical instrument: opportunity, exploration

N

natural disaster: challenge, resolution of trauma, apprehension, healing

net: trapped, constrained, complexity

noise: distraction, unrestrained, uncertainty

nudity: exhibitionism, vulnerability, loss, pride

nuts: assertive, uninhibited, balanced

O

ocean: opportunity, inner self, searching
open space: receptive, friendly

P

painting: self-enlightenment, tolerance, discovery
paralysis: frustration, fear of failure, hopelessness
party: social interest, pleasure
passageway: escape, journey, breakthrough
people: social interests, desire for social interaction
predator: dangerous impulse, debilitating hostility,
excessive aggression

Q

quarrel: frustration, dissatisfaction, conflict, arrogance
quietness: serenity, passivity, preparation, withdrawn

R

racing: impatient, motivated, reckless, thrill seeking
railroad crossing: caution, impending danger, unexpected
consequences
rain: enrichment, growth, cleansing
rainstorm: unrequited love, unfulfilled desires
road: the journey of life, new opportunities for growth
rock: unrelenting, determined, fixated
rocket: ambition, aggression, virility

S

sailing: progress, self-discovery

sanctuary: aspiration, spiritual opportunity, security

sand: calm, restrained, controlled

ship: adventure, transition, fate, destiny

shoe: material, earthly interests

shopping: self-nurturance, satisfaction of personal needs

singing: happiness, fulfillment, spontaneity, inner balance

skeleton: impoverishment of personal resource, fear of losing power

skidding: loss of control, excessive risk-taking

snow: reservation, reluctance, caution

snowstorm: vulnerability, indecisiveness, unpreparedness

stadium: social relationships, interest in social affairs, strivings for social acceptance

stairway: goal-related striving, planning, and problem-solving strategies

stone: stability, obstacle, adversity, resistance

struggle: inner conflict, fear, depression

sunburn: vulnerability to social pressure and repressed strivings

sunrise: new beginning, productive growth, personal enlightenment

swimming: strong survival drive, success in overcoming growth barriers

T

theater: fantasy, escape needs, inhibited motives or drives

timepiece: preoccupation with time

tomb: isolation, the unknown, personal loss

tombstone: fate and the inevitability of both good and bad consequences, the necessity of adversity in life

tower: ambition, self-reliance, independence, determination

toy: childhood, carefree, pleasure

train: inner growth functions, transitions, developmental progress

travel: change, growth, progress, discovery

tree: established, immovable, authority, capacity to generate and nourish life

truck: growth challenges

U

uniform: authority, conformity, power control

usher: conscience, spirit guide, security

V

vase: sensitivity, artistic, creativity

void: confusion, emptiness, meaninglessness

W

walking: conservative orientation, steady progress

war: internal conflict, struggle, turbulence, desperation

weapon: threat, aggression, hostility, frustration
web: trapped, helpless, constrained, struggle

Y

yacht: pleasure, adventure, journey
youth: optimism, accelerated growth, inquisitive orientation

Z

zoo: constraint, anxiety, discontent

References

Technical Reports, Athens State University Library Archives

TR-72, Dream Dynamics (1985)

TR-73, Creative Dreaming (1987)

TR-74, Creative Dream Intervention (1996)

TR-75, The Inspirational Dream (2003)

TR-98, OBES During Sleep (1986)

TR-99, Free Association (1992)

TR-101, Survey of OBEs (1990)

TR-102, Astral Travel during Sleep (1999)

TR-103, Advanced Astral Flow Program (1997)

TR-104, Out-of-Body Interactive Embracement (2003)

TR-105, Distant Partner Interactions (2001)

TR-106, Sequential Dreaming (1988)

TR-114, Extraordinary Dream Power (2002)

TR-115, Multidimensional Dream Power (1994)

TR-116, Extrasensory Dream Power II (1973)

TR-117, Clairvoyant Dream Power (1987)

TR-118, Dream Power Advancement Plan: Three Sequential Programs (1987)

TR-119, Hypnagogic/Hypnopompic Dream Intervention (1991)

TR-120, The Transcendent Stream (1983)

TR-121, The Transcendent Dream Element (1988)

TR-126, The Therapeutic Dream (1992)

TR-127, The Dream Embracement Program (1978)

TR-132, The Transcendent Dream Program (1988)

TR-133, Problem-Solving Power of the Transcendent Dream Element (1989)

TR-134, Transcendent Dream Activation Program (1990)

TR-135, Intellectual Power of the Transcendent Dream (1991)

TR-136, Health-Related Benefits of the Transcendent Dream (1991)

TR-137, Rejuvenation through Dream Power (2000)

TR-138, Therapeutic Potential of the Transcendent Dream (1993)

TR-139, The Problem-Solving Dream (1974)

TR-141, Analysis of Dream Journals (1987)

TR-150, Extraordinary Dimensions (2011)

TR-151, The Flowing With Procedure (1987)

TR-152, Dynamic Dream Power (1994)

TR-160, Dream Power Readiness Program (1996)

TR-171, The Precognitive Dream (1987)

TR-172, The Clairvoyant Dream (1987)

TR-173, The Telepathic Dream (1987)

TR-174, Retrocognitive Dream Power (1983)

TR-175, Comprehensive Dream Power Plan (1995)

TR-180, Dream Symbols (1987)

TR-188, The Finger-Spread Technique (1972)

TR-189, The 3-A Program (1995)

TR-191, The Five-Day Progressive Dream Power Plan
(2015)

TR-193, Orb of Energy Program (2015)

Bibliography

Arnold-Forster, Mary. 1921. *Studies in Dreams.* London:
George Allen & Unwin.

Slate, Joe H. 1988. *Psychic Phenomena: New Principles, Techniques, and Applications.* Jefferson, NC: McFarland & Co.
Inc.

———. 1991. *Self-Empowerment: Strategies for Success.* Bessemer, AL: Colonial Press.

———. 1997. *Psychic Empowerment: A 7 Day Plan for Self-Development.* St. Paul, MN: Llewellyn Publications.

———. 1999. *Aura Energy for Health, Healing & Balance.* St.
Paul, MN: Llewellyn Publications.

———. 2001. *Rejuvenation: Strategies for Living Younger, Longer & Better.* St. Paul, MN: Llewellyn Publications.

———. 2009. *Connecting to the Power of Nature.* Woodbury, MN: Llewellyn Publications.

Weschcke, Carl, and Joe H. Slate. 2009. *Psychic Empowerment for Everyone: You Have the Power, Learn How to Use It.* Woodbury, MN: Llewellyn Publications.

———. 2012. *Astral Projection for Psychic Empowerment: The Out-of-Body Experience, Astral Powers, and Their Practical Application.* Woodbury, MN: Llewellyn Publications.

———. 2015. *Communicating with Spirit: Here's How You Can Communicate (and Benefit from) Spirits of the Departed, Spirit Guides & Helpers, Gods & Goddesses, Your Higher Self and Your Holy Guardian Angel.* Woodbury, MN: Llewellyn Publications.

Acknowledgments

To all who participated in the production of this book, I wish to express my sincerest appreciation. I am especially grateful for the contributions of scores of college students and professional colleagues alike who gave their time and energy toward the pursuit of knowledge related to dream power. From voluntary personal reports of dreams to active participation in controlled laboratory studies, their participation became the essential core of this book.

To the coinvestigators and technicians who contributed tirelessly to our study of dream power and the dynamics related to it, I extend my sincerest thanks. Their grasp of the goals for this book from its beginning contributed immeasurably to a greater understanding of dream power as evidence based. The research results, including broad inferences of numerous high-impact studies, were to become an integral part of this book.

To the US Army Missile Research and Development Command, the Parapsychology Foundation of New York, and the Parapsychology Research Institute and Foundation (PRIF), I wish to express my sincerest appreciation for their interest in and support of research related to the discovery of new knowledge and its application

Finally, I owe an enormous debt of gratitude to the late Carl Llewellyn Weschcke, who remains commonly recognized worldwide as the Father of the New Age.

As his coauthor for numerous previous books, I will be forever grateful for the inspiration and enlightenment he consistently provided. His influence worldwide and beyond is unrelenting and will continue to evolve, time without end.

To Write to the Author

If you wish to contact the author or would like more information about this book, please write to the author in care of Llewellyn Worldwide Ltd. and we will forward your request. Both the author and publisher appreciate hearing from you and learning of your enjoyment of this book and how it has helped you. Llewellyn Worldwide Ltd. cannot guarantee that every letter written to the author can be answered, but all will be forwarded. Please write to:

Joe H. Slate PhD
℅ Llewellyn Worldwide
2143 Wooddale Drive
Woodbury, MN 55125-2989

Please enclose a self-addressed stamped envelope for reply,
or $1.00 to cover costs. If outside the U.S.A., enclose
an international postal reply coupon.

Many of Llewellyn's authors have websites with additional information and resources. For more information, please visit our website at http://www.llewellyn.com.